CREATIVITY

SIMPLE STEPS THAT CHANGE EVERYTHING

PATRICK FINN

Kendall Hunt

publishing company

Kendall Hunt
publishing company

www.kendallhunt.com
Send all inquiries to:
4050 Westmark Drive
Dubuque, IA 52004-1840

Copyright © 2011 by Kendall Hunt Publishing Company

ISBN 978-0-7575-9235-5

Printed in the United States of America
10 9 8 7 6 5 4 3 2 1

CONTENTS

ACKNOWLEDGMENTS

There are a lot of people to thank for this book. The first is Clem Martini who, along with the good people of the Teaching and Learning Fund at the University of Calgary, hired me to research, implement, and teach creativity classes. My debts to Clem have grown so large I don't know how they will ever be repaid.

Next are the advisors from every faculty on campus with whom I developed the creativity project so that it adequately addressed the needs of students from all parts of the university. Heather Smith-Watkins deserves special acknowledgement here.

Faculty members from Art, Dance, Drama, and Music helped with advice, readings, and feedback on the creation of the courses as well as with my ongoing research.

Margaret and Wendy from Kendall Hunt spearheaded the project and kept the fires burning throughout the process and made the whole thing fun!

Julie and Molly inspired me and put up with the long hours that it took to sift the information I wanted to try and share. My love to you both.

Finally, thanks to my students at the University of Calgary. They are the brightest bunch of people I have yet to encounter, and I am blessed to work with them.

Naturally, those mentioned above deserve the credit for all that is good about this book. Any errors, omissions, or overt foolishness is my responsibility alone.

Introduction

This book is simple. It is designed to meet you where you are. It is the result of several years of research and teaching at the University of Calgary, but also of decades of work in the performing arts and in public and private enterprise. Why read it? Governments and universities around the world are requiring students to study creativity as they come to realize the central importance of this subject. Also, it's fun.

This book is of its time. We are living in what has to be the most exciting period in history. The combined powers of globalization, digital technology, and various forms of research related to the brain make this an incredible time to be alive. It is also a time when it is essential to remain nimble in order to adapt to the surging changes that are carrying us along. The best way to promote this type of dynamic thought and action is to understand and enhance your creative powers.

This book is designed to help you. After reading all of the available work on creativity and performance I wanted to publish a short, simple book that would allow people to change the way they work with a small amount of effort. It is not that there are not other good books out there, it's just my understanding there is a need for a more direct approach to this essential work.

I have spent years working with artists in music, theatre, film, writing, design, dance, and multimedia arts, and there are a number of very simple things that I have observed that I believe will be of use to you. Moreover, I have worked for government and businesses that were interested in tapping into the same set of principles. The results of my research, firsthand experience, and interaction with students from every faculty at the university and from countries around the world has been collected and distilled here.

In case you do not have very much time, I will give you some of the most important ideas right now. First, you must recognize that you are already creative. If you find yourself disagreeing with that statement, you are wrong. Trust me, everyone is creative. We are creative in different ways, but we all have creativity running through us. It may be that it has not been nurtured or respected, but it is there, and this book will help you to come to terms with it.

Second, if you think you are a highly creative person and you have always felt that way, you may in fact be deluding yourself. Creativity is not a lifestyle, it is an ongoing practice, and chances are if you are doing the same types of things over and over again then your creative practice has gotten rusty. This book can help you, too.

Third, there are a few enemies of creativity that you will want to learn to avoid. Time is one of the first that comes to mind. High-pressure situations do not provide the best environment for creative work to occur. Judgment from self and others is an even more powerful one and can stop you before you even get started. Remember that creative work must be new by definition. As a result, anyone who knows you— and that includes you, yourself—may be taken aback when they see the things that emerge from working creatively. They just don't fit with the old you. You must develop a thick skin that allows you to continue even in the face of internal or external judgment.

There are two basic ways to study creative work. The first is the mentor model. In this model, we study creative people in order to emulate their work. In many forms of work, both past and present, systems are set up to allow students to benefit from the work of established figures. Building on this type of model, many people compile works that reflect on the creative processes of individuals or groups recognized for the quality of their work.

The other way to study creativity is through abstract analysis. In this model, we attempt to define the constituent parts of our topic and then replicate them in order to improve our own work. Studies of this type use comparisons between creative groups and individuals and often include studies that attempt to quantify the elements present in any given set of work. Both models have strengths and weaknesses. This book makes use of both models in an attempt to communicate most effectively and to provide checks and balances against the errors of one or the other model.

So, why should you bother to continue with this book? It is quite clear that in order to survive in a world that sees people switching jobs every two to five years it just makes good, practical sense. There are other reasons as well. We are now finding that people who pursue creative outlets at home and work are healthier. Tapping into the part of yourself that is closest to the true you is something that ends up being very effective at making us happier with our lives overall.

One of the main things that we end up finding out about creative practice is that we are often reluctant to give ourselves the time or space to express ourselves creatively. This—it turns out—is a bad decision. Freeing up the most dynamic parts of ourselves allows us to do more work in less time and to decrease stress in our emotional lives.

The good news is that working on your creative self can be a lot of fun. Study after study shows that highlighting your creative side will bring you pleasure. Sure, there are things that you can only access through some serious work, but anyone can make big changes with very little pain. Added to the fact that the work tends to be pleasurable is the unavoidable fact that the work itself is really quite simple. Minor modifications in what you are doing will give you immediate, measurable results.

This book will take you through an examination of a number of art forms. The reason for this is that professional artists are a natural source of learning about creativity. At their best, these people are expert tour guides through the realm of creativity. The reason for this is that creativity is at the heart of what they do.

We will also look at a number of different professions and paths because we need to learn that creativity works in all areas of our lives, and everyone can benefit from its growth. You will find that if you can begin to make a study of various creative events you will benefit from the information you gather. The benefits of studying those that are already working in a creative mode are double: first, we gain from the inspiration that such explorations offer and, second, we can learn from the practical work that these individuals use to reach us.

So what we are looking at is a good news/bad news situation. The bad news is that given what is currently happening to our world you simply cannot afford to sit still. In whatever way you choose to pursue your goals, you are going to be called upon to continually adapt along with a world that is changing faster every day. Those who do not find a way to engage with this new way of living will find themselves facing a tough future.

The good news is that the response to these changes is an expansion of a set of gifts we already have by using a process that is fun and easy. This book will show you how to do this right away. Think of it as preventative medicine. A little attention to this work will go a long way in keeping your personal and professional lives healthy.

Each chapter is short enough that you can read it quickly, and the organization is such that you can go through materials in whichever way you find works best for you. Along the way, I will provide you with simple assignments and questions designed to support your work. All I ask is that you try to follow along—if I am right, you will find that you experience changes almost immediately and then, over time, greater and deeper progress will follow. Thank you for picking up this book. Let's get started . . .

Creative People

The first thing we need to deal with is what I call the *creativity trap*. Over the past several years of teaching courses on creativity, this trap is the single largest impediment to the work that I have encountered. It goes like this—creative people walk around wearing outlandish clothes, observing some kind of strange diet (anything from vegan to nothing but cigarettes and red wine) and are always at all of the right shows, parties, and openings. Against this image we contrast the person in a suit. Clearly the first person is a creative, while the second is a mindless cog in a machine.

And there's the trap.

Creative people do not have a uniform. It is true that some creative folks use their particular way of dressing as part of their expression, but this does not apply to all or even most of the creative people you will encounter. The sooner you can come to terms with this the better. There are two reasons. The first is that spending time with creative people is good for your own work. So, the sooner you realize the difference between someone who is acting like an artist and someone who is genuinely creative the better.

The second—and more important—reason is that you need to take this lens off yourself. Time after time I have students come to me to talk about work in my class, and they start by saying "I'm not the creative type . . ." or, "I'm not artsy . . ." In my experience, this is just not true. Often, many of the best projects I get from my creativity courses come from folks that don't believe they are actually creative. It will be challenging and will take a little time, but you need to get over this thinking. You are creative, and your particular creativity needs to be the centre of your work. As such, you need to forget about trying to look or perform like people that appear to be artists and spend much more time on *your* unique creativity.

There are few things in life that are certain, but this is one: *you are already creative*. I promise. Therefore, all we are going to talk about is enhancing what you've got.

In real terms this means that we need to realize that creative people come in all types and work in every profession. Sure, there are some professions that make creativity a priority, but no background and no profession excludes creativity entirely. Moreover, in places where creativity is scarce, you can make big change if you are willing to work.

Now, we already have a bit of a problem. After all, if we just say everyone is creative the definition doesn't matter much. It's like saying everyone breathes—it doesn't really get us anywhere. But it does. Consider: we all breathe, but some of us work at improving our aerobic conditioning, some do breathing exercises and meditate, and others just let it happen. Creativity functions in the same way. It's there, but unless you work on it a bit you won't really be taking full advantage of it.

So, who is working on it? A lot of us.

You are living in a creative age. The way you and your fellow human beings work is more and more dependent on creative engagement. People that are creating new software, new models of philanthropy, medical breakthroughs, green technologies, television mini-series, live perform-ances, and new ways of organizing our cities continually have to re-invent the wheel. Those who can thrive in this fast-paced environment will be happy with the new state of being. Those who try to stick with past mod-els, which required less fluidity and provided more stability, will be in for a bit of a shock.

What do these creative people look like? They are the ones in the meeting that are not afraid to take risks. They don't mind trying new things, and they are almost always learning. Doesn't sound like you? Let's change that.

There is an old saying about courage that goes "courage does not mean that you have no fear, it means that you don't let fear stop you." Let's borrow that—creativity does not mean that you have no fear of fail-ure; it means that you go forward regardless of that fear. We'll spend more time on this later, but if you want to get started right away, here's a quick tip: You need to be doing things that are new and challenging in order to develop your creativity. That means that if you're the world's greatest poet or painter you don't need to write another poem or paint another picture as much as you need to explore another direction. It is that new horizon that will allow you to go further with your poetry.

Now, don't get me wrong, you still have to work—and work very hard—at your area of expertise in order to improve your craft. After all, every musician must learn their scales in order to perfect their craft, but to become an innovator, you have to exercise your complementary muscles.

Let me give you an example that may frustrate some of you. If you are one of the vast number of students that stopped taking math years ago, you need to work on your math muscles. You can start simple with some little number puzzles or a problem you can find online, but if you have let that part of your brain get lazy, then you are hurting your own potential.

Likewise—my friends in practical fields such as Engineering—if you haven't written a poem or done a finger painting in a decade or so you need to get back to it.

Pick things that are fun. Pick things that are small. Try a few things and then keep trying. If you get a little frustrated, that's probably a good sign—those muscles are weak. If you get really frustrated, then go easier on yourself. Pushing so hard that you quit within a few weeks will do more harm than never trying at all. It only helps you rehearse failure, which none of us should ever do.

Want some motivation? The folks that are doing this are going to take your job. Study after study shows us that lifelong learners are the ones that are continually employed and continually promoted. Watch the evening news sometime. Whenever they talk about shutting down a plant or a resource industry they interview people who thought their job would be there forever. Time after time we hear someone say, "I've been doing this all my life, I don't know how to do anything else." It's very sad because when they took those jobs the world was a place where people thought they could count on a stable job for a whole lifetime. Like it or not, that world is gone.

Now, I am not saying this is right or wrong. I am saying it is reality. Enhance your creativity or your life will be more difficult. Machines can do simple, repeatable tasks better than we can. Cheaper labor can take over jobs that require repetition and minimal initiative. To survive and thrive you need to enhance your life by switching on your own natural strengths. The best way to do this is to tap into your creativity.

Take a look around your world and notice those you think are successful. I guarantee they are creative people. They have to be in order to survive in today's world.

Finally, we have come to a bit of a warning. Creativity is neither good nor bad. It is what is called morally neutral. That means being creative can help you be a better dictator or drug lord the same as it can make you a better doctor or dancer. I make no promises about turning you into a more moral or ethical being—that is different work.

Here's your first task: pick five people you think are creative in different ways. List some of the ways they are creative. Make sure your picks are different. They don't have to be people you know, but try to pick at least one or two you know personally. Include someone who works in a field similar to yours. What can they teach you? What are they doing that no one else around them is doing? Keep your list for future work.

Creative Places

Right now governments and companies are falling all over themselves to try to find new ways to create spaces that promote innovation. This chapter will look at the importance of spaces that either promote or inhibit creative work.

Let's start with a thought experiment. If I were to ask you what a creative space looks like, what comes to mind? A cabin in the woods? A busy downtown café? A boat? A studio? A corner office? A backpack and no particular destination ahead? We all have different spaces that we would consider creative.

Let's do the opposite. What spaces inhibit creativity? Prisons? Countries that have undergone or are undergoing economic hardship? Places where you feel under threat? Of course, all of these make sense to us, but we will also find that some of the spaces listed as possible creative spaces also turn us off. These types of things are relative to the individuals who are judging them.

Two important realizations come out of this experiment. First, it is difficult to design a creative space that will work for all of the people you want to work with on any given project. Second, given the first realization, we had better be prepared to work in environments that have been created for someone else's idea of creativity.

Time for a reality check. Throughout this book, we are going to discuss ways to get in touch with your creative impulses and to enhance that area of your life. Often, I will use ideal scenarios for my examples, but we all know that ideals are just that—what we really need are a set of guidelines that work in the real world. It does not matter how much someone pays attention to providing you with a terrific work environment, it will almost always be a compromise, so get used to it and find ways to move forward. Waiting for the perfect creative space is a trap. Remember, Einstein worked in a patent office—the only true guarantee of creative work is doing the work.

Okay, so we have that out of the way. Now let's talk about creative spaces. A number of experts have worked on this issue over the last several decades. For obvious reasons different types of organizations—from armies, to software companies to design firms—all want to try and control space in a way that maximizes creative engagement in a way that is conducive to their particular goals. We can easily imagine some of the basics of this type of work—for example, dancers will need space to move and game designers will need high-end computers. The real spaces that matter, though, are two that we have very little control over. These spaces are our homes and our schools.

Studies demonstrate that those with homes that promote creativity end up with more creative children. That's not hard to imagine. So, why doesn't everyone do this in order to help their children? Well, it turns out it is not that simple.

You see, parents have a fundamental problem when it comes to creativity. The difficulty for them is that their primary interest for their children is safety. As such, they tend to advocate for stable choices that provide a high degree of predictability and stability over the long term. The motivations are nice enough, but as we discussed, the world no longer rewards the cog-in-the-machine worker, so if parents want to really help their children they are going to need to get on board with the creative revolution.

Another issue can relate to expectations. Households that have beliefs that a first-born child should do certain things or that males and females must perform very specific roles present challenges to the creative life. It doesn't necessarily prevent creativity, but it can certainly put up challenges to your work. The good news is that each of us also benefits from the unique nature of our upbringing. Even if that just means surviving a bad situation, you can use that in your work.

Much more dangerous than these general expectations is the over-critical household. If creativity is connected to everything innovative and of the future, criticism is connected to destruction and the past. Learn to recognize that criticism is fear with a mask.

Do you remember how I mentioned that creativity involves some form of risk? Well, the thing is that anytime we bring something new into the world it shakes up our view of the world we knew. That's why whenever someone develops a new artistic style, fashion, or means of working there are people that attack it with a passion. They are afraid, and there is nothing more dangerous to creativity than fear. If this example does not make sense to you then congratulations, you are in a supportive living environment. For many, though, any new work will be met with teasing and unhelpful judgment.

If this sounds like the type of treatment that only happens to us when we are young, it's not. This type of juvenile behavior follows us into all walks of life. Whenever you try something new you will open yourself to the attacks of those that are afraid of change of any kind. Be ready for it. If you grew up in a house like that, then I am truly sorry. It was not your fault, but you probably already know that you may struggle with that for the rest of your creative life. Remember, just use it and go forward. For those of you in mature relationships where your partner attacks your work, make a change. Either they learn and grow with you or you need to think about a new relationship. These folks are literally holding you back, and if you decide to tolerate it you are helping them pin you down.

The other foundational space is school. There is such a wide variety of instruction out there that it is hard to generalize. Certainly, it's always popular to say that school is broken and we need to radically change everything, but I think that's a bit of an overstatement. Things have been changing and they will continue to change. When I think of school I am reminded of Winston Churchill's comments about democracy. He said it was the worst form of government except for all the other kinds. Our education system is kind of like that—there are a lot of problems, but overall we are quite fortunate.

As someone who has spent a significant amount of time studying schools let me suggest a way that you can maximize your time or that of your children. First, look at the best schools—that is, where do rich folks who can pick whatever they want send their children? The answer is a school with arts and sciences and lots of extra-curricular activities. I don't need to teach a medical student at Harvard that they need courses focusing on creativity—they already have to take them as part of their degree.

If you cannot afford to buy a great education, then you will need to make one for yourself. That means keeping diversity in your studies and finding ways to do meaningful extra-curricular work. It's up to your parents when you are young; it is up to you once you've grown up.

So here is the reality. If our education system really delivered a full spectrum education to all of us we would all be more creative, but we do not have the resources to do that. Education funding is limited. Classes are getting larger and fewer teachers are being employed. That's just the way it is. If you want to have any hope of functioning in the world in which you are working, you had best understand that you are going to need to go out and get your education. You need to be a lifelong learner, and you need to take charge of your educational workouts. Over-train one area and you will be out of balance.

So, what is a creative space? It is a place that does more to promote than to inhibit creativity. Where are they? They are wherever you are—you make them yourself.

Here's your task: describe one space that inhibits your creativity and one that helps it.

Some **4** Definitions

Alright, it is probably time to try and come up with a working definition of creativity. If you have already been asking "isn't creativity different for different people?" then you know we will need an agreed-upon understanding if we hope to continue.

Let's get to it. Why don't we start by cherry-picking the material we have already covered and then add things as we go? Following are seven positives and one negative.

Creativity is amoral. It won't make you better or worse as a person, though it almost certainly will make you better at what you do. Most of those who work on creativity assert that getting in tune with the productive side of life will actually cause us to become better people, but we can't really establish this, so let's leave this alone for the time being.

Creativity is universal. At least as far as our understanding goes, we all have creativity within us. We may not be using it—actually, we may even be doing our best to crush it—but it is there.

Creativity is granular. If we accept that creativity is universal than we have to find ways to distinguish between highly developed creativity, dormant creativity, and all points in between. We may also find that this fluctuates within us at different points in our lives. While we may not be able to come up with a creativity metric, we can surely speak in general terms about more or less creativity being present. This component will allow us to distinguish creative work on a small project and the type of creativity that gives rise to a major, historic discovery.

Creativity is multiple. I would like to suggest that we have multiple creativities within us. Consider an example—you are a huge success at work. Everyone around you worships the ground you walk on because you continue to innovate and explore new areas. Yet, at home, your relationship is stuck in the mud, and you treat your kids like your parents treated you, and you treat your partner the way your parents treated each other. What we see here is that highly developed creativity in one area of a life may not carry over to other areas.

Creativity is relative. We all judge creativity differently. In my experience, the quickest way to get at an example of this is to ask people about their favorite music or movies. We very quickly find that one person's art is another person's trash. Whether or not we want to accept the idea that anyone can judge all forms of creativity and usefully comment, we can certainly agree that we all have our own opinions on these types of issues.

Creativity is new. Whatever our differences, we can all agree that to create, innovate, or explore involves finding something new. It may be a new way of looking at old things or ideas, but newness has to be in there somewhere.

Creativity has value. Try not to think of this only as money. Value simply means that whatever has been created means something to someone. It has causality. The most important thing to understand here is that it does not need to have primary relevance. That means that just because you cannot put a dollar value on the discovery you just made in your performance art piece does not mean it has no value. In fact, it is more likely that truly creative work will have more complicated values than things that have immediate-use value. Projects geared to immediate-use value tend to be the least creative projects with which we engage.

Okay, we've got some pretty good positive terms; next we will try an important negation.

Creativity does not come from a vacuum. This statement means that it is nearly impossible to find something that is entirely original because all of our learning and expression are based on things we have learned which have come to influence us. Just how much borrowing someone does will determine how creative or original we determine the work to be, but we need to realize that everyone has influences.

My guess is that you are already recognizing just what it will take to define creativity. When we look at all the research and consider what we have said, we end up with something like this:

Creativity involves making something new that has value.

I hope we can agree on that much. If not, let's look at our biggest challenges. The two main words in that sentence are *new* and *value*. Both of them end up coming down to matters of debate. If you listen to a new song just released and think it is new, but I think it is a rip-off of an earlier artist, how do we decide who is right? The answer is it will take a great deal of discussion, and we may never reach a resolution; however, it seems that we can agree that the *newness* is crucial to the creative enterprise.

That second word is just as tricky. Who gets to determine value? There has been an argument about this going on in societies around the world for as long as people have been thinking and debating. At some times and in some places experts were used to establish value. Thus, one critic might tell us that one painting is a masterpiece and the other that it is not worth the time to examine.

The difficulty is that any system of experts carries its own problems. In our world of seemingly infinite information it sure seems like a good idea to have experts help to point us toward things we really ought to experience. The challenge comes when interests that complicate the process sway those in places of cultural power. Thus, at certain times countries want their citizens to believe certain things that will benefit the government. In such circumstances, arts organizations and funders might move support towards those things that are deemed beneficial by those in power. Again, this is a debate that is not going to be easily—if ever—resolved; however, all of us can agree that in order to qualify as being truly creative the notion of value must come into play. Otherwise, the creative practice is emptied of any relevance in the world.

Our definition is quite broad, and it needs to be that way. In order to avoid the creativity trap, we need to understand that creativity happens in cubicle farms, kitchens, fields, studios, and alleyways. Further, in order for us to have a useful discussion about all creative manifestations, we need a definition that will permit a broad study.

Let's test our definition with a couple of examples.

Albert Einstein's Theory of Relativity drew on the thinking of his predecessors and was developed in conjunction with others who were thinking of related ideas, but it was undeniably a new way of looking at available information. His work on that theory continues to inform the study of physics and has even come to influence our popular culture through a more general knowledge of his contributions.

William Shakespeare's use of the soliloquy connects to earlier traditions of theatre and was developed in conjunction with work by contemporaries, such as Christopher Marlowe, but it also fundamentally changed the way theatre was practiced and went on to influence the way people's minds have been described in our culture.

Both examples are certainly open to debate, but both involve the creation of something *new* that is of *value*. I hope we can agree to use this definition for our discussions.

Your task: test our definition for yourself. Keep a record of your results.

Creativity and the Arts

When you study creativity one of the areas that you have to be careful with is the arts. We often think that art means creativity or vice versa, and it is simply not the case. The arts are an area where creativity should be the prime concern, but this is not always the way things work out. That said, one of the main reasons I wrote this book is because there are not very many books on creativity that are written by artists. Educators, business gurus, and social scientists write a lot of them, but most artists seem to be too busy working on their art-specific projects to take up the subject.

With this warning in mind, I want to suggest that the arts still retain the central position in any consideration of creativity. They are the only area that has consistently placed creativity at the centre of their work. In this book, we will look at a number of the older arts traditions and then at the new world of art that is seeing the old groups merge. New technology and new collaborations are causing the old areas of theatre, painting, dance, and music, for example, to collapse into various hybrids of performance art.

What do you think of when I say "the arts?" Is the phrase positive or negative for you? The biggest discovery I have had in my work with students in creativity class is that many people feel that the arts are alien to them. I think that's a great sign. If you go to a performance and you feel like you just don't *get it* that is very good news. The reason is that our creative selves benefit greatly from being unsettled.

Take a second and think about it. If what we are after is finding ways to be continually fluid in our thinking, what better way than to find something that unsettles us? At the same time, I would suggest that if you are someone who attends so many arts events that you are no longer startled out of your everyday mode of thinking, then you need to cut back and go and experience other things. For most of us, though, we are going to want to increase our exposure to the arts.

Earlier in the book I promised you that this exploration would be fun. It will be, but I should warn you that if you are unused to attending arts events you might feel a little awkward at first. Once you get over that, things should be a lot more fun.

When we look at creativity research, practice-based models almost always suggest that you program into your calendar a series of arts events that are meant to inspire you. That is a great idea, but you will need to modify it for your own reality. We should talk about how you do that, but first let's talk a bit on practice-based models.

You will recall that I mentioned that one of the two main ways to study the arts is the mentorship model. Practice-based models follow in that tradition. The great news about following this type of program is that it is very easy to understand and implement. The argument here is that you benefit merely by being exposed to different types of experiences. There are a number of abstract reasons for this, but scientifically we now know that we learn through watching or experiencing. Those of you that have worked on sports or music programs that follow mentor models will be familiar with this type of work. For the rest, you will understand what I am talking about as soon as you do it.

In order to follow this model you need to plan to experience some form of art on a regular basis. If you are completely jammed this might only be once a month, but if you can, once a week is a better idea. Here's the tough part. You can't do what you already do. If you are already seeing a lot of movies, you should probably not use movies as your work. Try to find something that you do not normally do and attend it.

Some general ideas are trips to art galleries, plays, dance shows, music recitals etc. There is no shortage of these types of events, and you should be able to find something that is affordable in your area. If you cannot, you can cheat and go online and watch something from these areas, but remember that live is better. Cheaper and easier options are the reading of poetry, short stories, graphic novels, or other such items. Again, you should try and choose things that you do not usually experience. That means that at first you may feel a little discomfort at the idea of the experience. That's a good sign—follow it.

Why should you follow discomfort? Didn't I promise you that this would be fun? The reason is one of the most important things that you will ever read and is at the heart of everything I have discovered in my work on creativity and performance. Here it is . . .

Creative people don't judge.

Sounds simple, right? It is one of the most important things that I have noticed when I have worked in business, the arts, government, and education. The truly creative people move past the desire that we all have to mock things they do not understand and to devalue things that cause discomfort.

If you want to be more creative—and this I guarantee you—one of the most crucial things you can do is to drop your critical mind. Every successful person I know follows this approach. It means that you have to work hard not to turn off and ignore a performance that you do not understand. It is absolutely fine not to understand. People who tell you they understand everything are lying. Get over the need to make sense of everything—remember, that weird feeling of being moved out of your comfort zone is what we are after. At the same time, you have to avoid going to the other extreme and just praising the heck out of everything. Try instead to take it all in—just experience the work. All you have to do is try to stay awake and learn from what is happening. You don't have to like it, and you don't have to be able to translate it. Just be there.

The best I can do by way of example is to explain something from my own life. I am someone who always loved music. At an early age, I began to follow certain performers. I knew who played on what recordings, and I knew a lot of details about their lives. I knew which artists I liked and which artists I did not like, and I could tell you in detail.

Then I became a musician and something changed. Once I worked at the craft and became a professional, I dropped all those lists and needs to rank various artists. I became more curious about the work, and I began to see things in all artists that were worth studying and learning from in order to improve my work. The same thing happens to people who work in any profession.

So let's be clear—this works in all professions and practices. Whether you are in business, engineering, sports, or medicine, the more you want to excel the more you will be fascinated by how others practice your discipline. Again, you do not have to *like* them or their work, but you can learn from what they do.

Now let's extend this finding. Research tells us that our work expands and strengthens when we work other aspects of our thinking. So, if we go to an art exhibit and we have never been to one before and we feel awful while we are there (imagine you are there and you say in our head, "this is crap") that's actually the best sign you can have—that's pain coming from the muscles of your mind. That's the discomfort you get when you work a muscle that has never been worked before . . .

Let's follow this metaphor a little further. If you go to that same art opening and all you ever do is go to art openings—you know everyone, you know the artist, their influences and everything else—you will feel comfortable and at ease. That's the sign that you no longer need to focus on those muscles. Could be that you need to go to an entirely different event that will make you uncomfortable in order to learn.

Your task: plan some arts events into your schedule and attend them without judgment.

Creativity and History

One of the best ways to study creativity is through the lens of history. There are many reasons that this is the case, but two very different approaches provide immediate interest. Putting things in the order in which they occur is an easy way to organize a set of ideas or arguments. Some people like this approach and some do not, but you cannot argue with its effectiveness.

Another great idea—at least from my perspective—is that we can evaluate the movement of history through the lens of creativity. History tends to focus on our perceived existence on this planet. As such, we can access various movements or developments based on their connections to creativity. In the most general sense, we can talk about all of history as the record of creative enterprises.

So, let's start at the beginning. When we study the world through the creative lens we have to look at what are called "creation myths." That is, stories from societies around the world that describe the creation of life on earth and all of the other things that go into those considerations. Now, I don't want to go into religion here. In my experience it is a topic that can be very useful for creativity, personally, but it is a real conversation killer when you try to discuss it generally. That is because a lot of us have set beliefs that we are not willing to question or have questioned. As such, it's an area that is of no use to a general discussion of the creative.

Taking the sacred out of the discussion, and merely focusing on the narrative of creation, we can quickly agree that all parts of the earth have stories about how we got here, how the planet got here, and how the creative force behind those events operates. Indeed, these creation stories are almost always among the first stories that we find from any given people.

Those of us that are interested in creativity find that we end up with a world that seems to be designed or brought into being by creativity. In many cases, we find that the description involves the only act of creativity that comes out of nothing and into something. Thus, we find ourselves in a world that was created by a being or process greater than ourselves, which has left us the tools to continue on by example.

Evidence of creative work crops up around the world, and we often look at such things as cave paintings as evidence that we have been creative beings for as long as we have been thinking. Once we begin thinking like this we end up running into an issue that historians know very well. Can we look at creativity as progressing over time? That is, when we create, do we take the art that came before us and make something that is somehow better or more advanced or is it just different? The answer ends up being pretty important to the way we think about creativity but also about humanity in general.

Following the idea that we are developing, we can view the world as a place in which our talents have continued to improve as we have tried different modes of expression. If we take the larger view of our timeline, this line of thinking allows us to see ourselves as beings that gradually began to create, bringing ourselves into line with the forces that brought us into being in the first place. If you take this view—and many do—you might then also find that you think that we have peaks and valleys. That is, you might think that painting, for example, was better at a certain point and then began to fall off or lose direction only to find its way again at a later point.

If you do not like your history in long lines, you can take it in big lumps instead. Thus, you can merely examine artistic movements in terms of their specific time and draw out conclusions from there. The obvious choices here are periods like the European Renaissance or Pre-Columbian art in Mexico and Central and South America. Here, again, we can attach judgments about the importance or potency of these periods and seek for reasons that the creative work of these times was what it was.

So, let's take a look at the two biggest outcomes of a historical look at creativity.

If we use the model that our world came into being through the creative forces of some being beyond us, then our drive to create can be directly connected to a holy figure that we may wish to both emulate and honour. This model has a lot of supporters and turns up a great deal of research.

Throughout the world, we find creative works that are done and dedicated to a superior life form. These creations would not have happened were it not for the desire of those people to honour the being from which they came. Connected to this we also have a huge volume of work that is done by individuals and groups that feel they were directly inspired or infused with creative impulses from their creator.

In these traditions, there are also rules and debates over what types of creations are appropriate and which might not be. Some people feel that an artistic reproduction of certain figures should be prohibited, while others think that it is a loving tribute. We will not solve these debates, but we can certainly recognize that creativity is important in both these streams of history.

In the second stream, creativity is part of a natural set of evolutionary traits that has been favoured through thousands of years of trial and error. Here, again, engaging in the creative spirit connects to whatever life force gives us our existence. Large numbers of people have seen creative work as experimentation that allows us to participate in the evolution of our species—to test various traits and engage with their selection or deletion.

In a fascinating coming together of the spiritual and scientific views, a whole field of creative work that explores questions of creation has sprung up. This area of exploration looks at the tensions between natural and human creation. One of the more famous examples is Mary Shelley's *Frankenstein*, a book that explores interesting questions about science and reproduction, the benefits of literacy, and the alienating effects of academic pursuits. Works of this kind explore questions we have about how our creativity lines up with the creative forces of the world in which we find ourselves.

The final observation on this level is a trend that we see around the world. This trend sees the feminine with a special connection to creativity. Whether in myth, religion, or science the idea of the female as the primary force in the creation of life is a shared history. The debates around this are fierce and fascinating, but whatever our personal position, we can certainly see that they are important in all cultures.

So, are there any general statements we can make about history and creativity? We can certainly make an argument for saying that history charts the movement of creative forces, but we cannot go so far as to promote it as a unifying principle. All societies engage with this type of history but do so in such vastly different ways that no agreement is likely.

It seems that all societies agree in some way that the forces we exercise when we are being creative connect to the same type of power that is at play when we ourselves came into being. We may have different explanations for those primary forces, but we all agree that they are creative at heart. It seems to me that this is quite a powerful statement. It seems that our history is fundamentally connected to creativity as a means of our production and as something that provides us with inspiration and in some way calls us to connect with something outside ourselves in order to engage with those larger creative forces in some fundamental way.

Your task: take a few moments and write out what you believe to be the true nature of creative energy and how this connects to your creative work. Keep your notes.

Creativity and Theory

This chapter scares me. Here's why: theory is an ongoing interest of mine. I've taught it at university and read a mountain of it. Yet, it remains a highly controversial area of study and for very good reason. At its best, theory provides a set of tools for engaging with culture that fosters insights well beyond anything possible without an awareness of its operations. At worst, it is a watered down form of philosophy that shuts down all useful conversation in the name of self-indulgent musings. With the exception of religion it is the single most troublesome subject area for someone wishing to discuss creativity. So, with that harsh warning in place here we go . . .

First, I will try and take a crack at explaining what theory is . . .

Whenever you want to go about examining something new the best thing to do is to try and get at what the elements you are studying are made of. The word *theory* comes from the Ancient Greek and basically means something that is under study in an abstract way. This definition contrasts with the Greek term for *practice*, which was to study something in application. For those of you interested in university education, theory is at the heart of academic study and practice is at the heart of professional study. So, a traditional academic will look at the theory of bridge architecture and an engineer will look at how that bridge was actually made. Both are essential, but we are focusing on theory for now.

Theory nowadays is universally recognized as a way of engaging with information that developed out of several disciplines beginning mostly in the 1960s and peaking in the 1980s and 1990s. The work continues, but during those decades theory dominated the way that several central disciplines within the academy operated.

Many different disciplines contributed, but I think it is safe to say that much of it centred on what was called the *linguistic turn*. This phrase referred to a new study of the way in which language works. Scholars from anthropology, history, literature, the arts, philosophy, linguistics, and all of the social sciences, as well as some of the pure sciences, began to pay more attention to the fine details of words and how and why they were used.

The arguments that surrounded this work were highly charged and led to some real battles over ideas that split quite a few academic departments. Work in this area has cooled over time, but theory has now earned a place as an area of expertise that students have to take account of in order to get their degrees. You can think of theory like nuclear power. It has incredible potential but in anything other than expert hands it's just plain deadly.

So, why does this matter to us?

First, we should be aware that theorists have a stake in the creativity game and we want to be aware of that, but second, and more importantly, theory offers us a great opportunity to learn more about our topic. I've thought a lot about this and what I want to do is to send you on a theoretical journey through creativity rather than just giving you a theoretical reading of our topic.

Our journey begins with a split. It will be very general, but I want to divide all of theory into two types. The first we will call *formal*, and the second we will call *cultural*. Formal theory takes a look at the constituent components of any given expression in order to unearth hidden meaning. Cultural theory looks at all of the societal, historical, political, and other such areas that contribute to any given expression and studies them for deeper meaning.

On the first side of the split what you want to do is conduct an investigation into the way in which I have defined creativity. Remember that we said that it was something like this:

"Creativity involves making something new that has value."

Read that sentence like it is a puzzle. Look up all of the words in the dictionary and list all of the meanings and the meanings of the roots of the words. Try to decipher any hidden messages that might be in the formulation that I have put forward. Doesn't sound exciting enough? Imagine you are in a crime drama. The writer of a new creativity book has lost his mind while writing a chapter on theory and has taken your family hostage. I have them in a barn, and I won't release them. I send you the previous message in a ransom note. Figure it out and I'll send them back. Until you solve the puzzle, I will keep them tied up and read theory to them out loud as they cry hopelessly for help.

What you will find, if you take the time, are a series of avenues of meaning that can give you insight into the topic, the way I wrote it, and even your own position of interpretation.

Now, let's try the other side of the split. On the opposite side from the linguistic is the cultural. This lens is broader and comes at our sentence from another angle. There are also a lot more questions to ask. Let's look at a few different approaches.

Do you think it is possible that people from two different cultures might interpret the word *value* differently? What about one person who is poor and one person who is rich? A man and a woman? Someone who is homosexual? Do you think that a musician who just released a song that sounds a lot like an old song that is no longer protected by copyright is creating something new? Will a liberal and a conservative both view *newness* in the same light?

My guess is that you will answer these questions the same way most of us do, "yes, no, maybe, and everything in between." They are simply too big to satisfy with simple answers. But I am also willing to bet that you can see right away that these questions do raise important considerations for our study. Theorists spend their time articulating these questions in order to tease out the underlying information behind such formulations. For our part, let's do this exercise: take the word *creation*. What does it mean to you? To your ancestors? To those of your economic group? Gender? Sexual predisposition? Notice how these questions quickly unearth discrepancies in the way we might discuss a simple proposition like, "creativity involves making something new that has value."

So what can theory do for us? It comes down to what you want it to do. On the one hand, it can help us to better understand the way we define and study creativity. One the other hand, if we get too mired down in questions that are ancillary to what we are after then it has to be discarded as an impediment to our work.

At the start of this book I promised you that we would keep our work simple. That means we need to keep to the path of least resistance. I am starting from the assumption that the vast majority of people that read this book will be very busy. As such, you probably want to get at the heart of the matter right away and begin working on your own creativity. That's what we will continue to do, but always be aware that going back and deepening your theoretical approach to this work will provide you with opportunities to dig a little deeper into the topic.

By way of example, if you are the curious type imagine the sorts of things you could unearth if you did a close examination of the language and cultural components of my statement in an earlier chapter that "creativity is amoral." You could spend a lifetime following all of the possibilities. Of course, that's not our purpose in this book, so we are going to continue our quest.

Your task: keep the answers you came up with for the two exercises in this chapter.

Creativity and Education

Education is one of the most important areas in creativity research. For obvious reasons, the places and methods that we use to teach our children and ourselves have direct impact on whether or not we develop our creative skills. If you learn only one thing from this chapter, let it be this: for creativity, you need to be a lifelong learner.

There are a few things that we need to deal with before getting to the most important aspects of creativity in education. I will be summarizing huge bodies of research, so I apologize for being brief, but being brief is what this book is all about! I'm going to call this little section "truth in education." It's a bold claim, but I've been at this for a long time now and I think I can back up what I say.

First, almost everyone thinks that there is a crisis in education. Some think it's too easy, some think it's too hard. Some think there is too much money in it; some think there is too little. Every year we hear new theories about why education is broken and how it must change in order to meet the demands of today. Here's the truth—we are actually doing pretty darn well overall. There are huge areas that need improvement, but we've been working at education for years and there have been huge advances. The thing is that education is so important that people interested in arguing about it get quite passionate and, in order to be heard, they use the "sky is falling" method. In this approach, only the one who shouts loudest gets heard.

Second, you are responsible for your own education. I alluded to this earlier, but it is truer than ever. Your parents or guardians are on the hook for this when you are young, but by the time you hit upper grade school some of this responsibility is already going to be off-loaded on to you. Why do I keep harping on this responsibility? Universal education.

Universal education is a great thing. It means that we all go to school. It also means that your teachers are overwhelmed by the huge amount of variation in the students they are supposed to teach. Two basic outcomes can be produced here. A teacher who can tap into all that variety can give you access to a dynamic learning environment. If, however, the room is out of control and the only way to keep things from turning into a full-out riot is to impose a homogenized program of work, you are going to get the worst part of universal education—teaching to the average. The whole notion of average is anathema to creativity.

Third, Aristotle was right—"we are what we repeatedly do." If you find yourself trapped in a bad educational environment and you decide to swim with the current, you will be training yourself for mediocrity. Is that fair? Who can say? What I can tell you is that if you are interested in creativity, you are going to have to get involved with your own educational path. That's just the way it is.

Fourth, you need to think long term. Your education—along with your physical and emotional health—are the best long-term investments you will ever make. Don't waste your time. The biggest obstacle you will face to this truth is the hype that comes from certain governments and certain schools that are trying to satisfy short-term needs in specific job areas. Do not listen to them. Train yourself for a lifetime of work, not for a pre-defined job.

Fifth, be rich. Okay, that's out of your control, but I will tell you the best way to survive the current educational system. If you are born rich this has already been taken care of for you. If you are like most of us though you are going to need to pretend you were born with more money and as a result have more choices.

Take a look at the types of schools people send their kids to when they have a choice. They all have arts programs, athletics programs, organized, extra-curricular activities, and strict academic requirements. You can get the same education in the real world, but only if you force yourself to live by the same rules that people who have choice do. Science tells us that working more areas of your brain makes you smarter. So do it. You don't need to pursue things you do not like—find things that attract you, but make sure you are getting a balanced educational diet. Any counselor that advises you to drop classes that you find challenging should be ignored.

I am sorry if this sounds kind of harsh, but I wanted to make sure that I gave you the secret to getting a great education. A good education will not come and get you. You have to go out and get it.

So, what does this have to do with creativity? Everything. In order to be nimble minded, in order to have the best chance at innovation, discovery, and the creation of new ideas, you have to start from a strong foundation. Your foundation is your education. We know from study after study that if you want to get the most out of school you need to: move around, practice the fine arts, academically study arts and sciences. Add to this multiple literacies—as in letters, numbers, and the newer multimedia literacies. If you go to a great private school, this is all taken care of for you. If you don't, you need to take care of this on your own.

Do you want an example of this private school argument? In Canada, our government gives funding to Catholic School Boards to run their own schools—aptly titled Separate Schools. Many of you that went to Catholic schools will know one of the best-kept secrets in education. Most of the kids in Catholic schools are not practicing Catholics, but are instead the children of parents that want to try and get an education that is more like private school for their kids. The reason? In the past, Catholic schools tended to have more art, more sport, stricter academic guidelines, and more rules. It's not my place to say whether or not this is a good idea, but it is certainly an example of parents trying to access the type of education I am telling you about.

At this point, you are probably wondering why I am hitting you with all of this scary stuff. The reason is that part of living in the most interesting time so far in history means you live in a time of change. Do not listen to people who say that the world is changing. It has already changed. It will take a while for our large systems to adjust to that, but in the meantime you need to live your life. You do not want to be a footnote to history.

Think about the type of job you want to have. If it is non-creative, a machine can do it. The first jobs that went were manufacturing, but now it is accounting, engineering, and medical work that is evaporating. Where I live, our parents grew up in a world where a diploma or degree could guarantee lifetime employment. That is no longer the case. For years, we have been reading about jobs going overseas. The companies that outsource are doing quite well financially. What incentive do they have to bring jobs back? None. Lifelong jobs are not coming back. You have to make them.

To me, the most important message that I can give to university students—and they are the ones that I work with—is that if you are not working hard at being a student you need to quit. A degree with no real direction and no extra-curricular work is worse than nothing. Remember Aristotle's principle: *"you are what you repeatedly do."* If all you do is hang around doing nothing for four years and get your degree without ever really engaging, you've just become an expert at being a drain. Don't be surprised if no one wants to hire you to come hang around their company and collect a check.

Okay, so now you are terrified and ready to leap off the nearest building. But don't—the solution to all of this is a happy one. You just have to get creative. I've been ranting at you about lifelong education and you need to hear that, but the good news is that the types of things you need to do can be fun.

My guess is that most of the people that are reading this book are already working too hard. You do not need to work harder; you just need to get creative. When we look at the research, we see that students who throw in a bit of music, or painting, or dance perform better on their other tasks. You don't have to become an expert at the other discipline, just add a dash of it—sort of like adding a little spice to your recipe. The opposite of this is also true—if you do nothing but arts, you need to explore some math and science. Every major university in the world is beginning to put course materials online for free—browse them. Learn something new every day. A little effort in a discipline you do not normally practice will free your mind up to function in a more creative way.

Two rules should guide you through this—1) never accept the opinion of anyone who tries to limit your explorations, and 2) try not to be dismissive of new information that is so challenging it makes your head hurt a bit. Those are just your muscles growing!

Your task: analyze *your* education. Are there areas you have neglected? Take one tiny step towards addressing that area.

Creativity and Health

Get creative and it will improve your health, it's as simple as that. I am sure that you have heard of someone using art to help people that are suffering from some kind of physical, psychological, or emotional condition. People have used plays to help groups heal past conflicts, painting to help individuals express repressed feelings, writing to explore various forms of trauma, and on and on. Anyone who has ever sung along with a powerful song that somehow seems to help capture their feelings knows that there is power in artistic expression.

We also know from neurological studies that regions of the brain can be usefully stimulated by work with the fine arts. Certain types of patients with neurologic disorders can be calmed using sculpture, music, and painting. Still others can be helped to recover from brain injury using similar tactics. We also know that engaging in something expressive can be an excellent way to relieve stress. This latter effect can hardly be overvalued given that stress is one of the biggest threats to our health today.

All of this is to say that creative endeavors are good for your health. For our purposes, let's leave the solving of major health issues to the professionals. What we are concerned with is our own creative lives. We're making a double move here, so we better make sure we stick to our original proposition.

In an earlier chapter we established that creativity involves "creating something new that has value." Now here comes the trick—if I come home from work after my boss has been treating me horribly and I take out a huge sheet of newsprint and some finger paints and I paint a picture of him and then smush paint all over his face, it's not very likely that the resulting "painting" is going to bring in the big bucks at a gallery. Sure, you could say that *if* it helps me to calm down after a tough day at the office then it has *value* for me, but really that's getting kind of nitpicky.

What we will find is that engaging with *entirely* creative work – which is very often, but not always something drawn from what is known as the *fine arts*—will give us health benefits. You can laugh all you want at my painting example, but stress is killing people in droves. It shreds our bodies from the inside and yet has no physical presence. (What I mean by this is that you can't pick up "stress" on any kind of scan.)

So, I can come home and stew over my evil boss and bicker with anyone who is around me, or I can do my painting experiment, have a good laugh, and move on. Sounds silly, right? Well, so what? Who ever said silly was a bad thing anyway? But, don't take my word for it—try it once. If it doesn't work, not only don't you ever have to do it again, but you can say you honestly tried it rather than being one of those creativity cowards that never does anything except give reasons why other people's creative experiments are silly (which we know is a mask for their own fear anyway!).

And here comes the big point. When we think of leveraging our creativity for better health we need to revisit the term *value* in our definition of creativity. If you go home tonight and write a poem, compose a song, do a dance, try a new recipe, or do a finger painting none of them have to be "good" in order for them to help you develop your creativity. In fact, the single most important thing you can learn about creativity and health is to get away from first-order thinking that causes you to want to judge that way.

What's first-order thinking you say? It's basing your decisions on simple cause and effect. If you only ever do things because they make sense in first-order thinking you will trap yourself. One of the biggest reasons to avoid first-order thinking is that any computer can outdo humans at this type of non-creative thought. The biggest reason is that first-order thinking just doesn't make sense in the real world. The problem is that it is just so easy to think in these terms that we often slip into it unintentionally.

Let me give you an example. Imagine a young kid in class. He's not paying attention to the teacher who is taking the class through some basic mathematics. Now, we know that the kid is going to be better off if he learns his math, so what do we do? First-order thinking only allows us to consider the math, so we force him to do the math. If that doesn't work, we find some way of forcing him to sit still. How well do you think that is going to work?

What if, instead of forcing him to do the math, we run him around the playground doing something physical for the hour before the math lesson? We know that exercise improves both thinking and physical well-being. Problem is, running around does not connect to math in first-order thinking.

Now, imagine you are in charge of that kid's school. Business and government ask you to raise math scores. You have limited funds, so you cut physical education and increase funding to mathematics. That is classic first-order thinking. You may get brownie points for responding to the request you got, but in the long run you are harming that kid and actually moving further from the results you want.

I want to leave this abstract example, but before I do I should make one last note. We also need to remember that physical education benefits from creative thinking as well. That means physical education should be dynamic and based on things that engage the kids. If they want to dance instead of doing gymnastics we need to find ways to meet them where their passion lies. (Sorry, I just had to throw that in because I hated a lot of the options I had in gym class as a kid.)

If using creativity can improve our health, we need to test that against our real-world experience. When we do this we can identify three general areas of health: physical, mental and emotional. We have plenty of studies that tell us that if you add some creative time to your life your stress level will come down, your mental acuity will improve, and your overall emotional well-being will benefit, but of course, you need to test those things for yourself.

My guess is that the biggest impediment to getting you working on this is that you are already so busy that taking the time to do a finger painting experiment will seem beyond your means. That was only an example. Here's the trick—take a look at your past and jot down any activities that you used to do that you've dropped in order to spend more time on your studies or on work. Chances are there are a bunch of things that you used to do that would actually be beneficial to your current goals.

Your list might include things as disparate as gardening, knitting, model building, animal training, martial arts, dance, brain-teasers, or baking. One of the truly fascinating things about our creative impulses is the sheer power of their being. Even if you have covered them up, they will pop up. Perhaps your drawing has become doodling on the block of paper at your desk, or your writing has become clever jokes or posts in one of the various online communities. Find these things you stopped doing and bring one back. Do it for fifteen minutes a day.

Here's a warning. If you are a true workaholic, which seems to be an almost universal disease at this point, you might feel that these fifteen minutes are a waste of time. Remember, that is first-order thinking. Those fifteen minutes are an investment in your health in both your personal and professional lives. Chances are, once you see the benefits that will follow this experiment, you will expand those fifteen minutes to an hour or two a day, but start small so that it is easy to do.

The other major tactic that you need to remember is the addition of nourishing events. That means getting out of the office or your house and doing things that you have not done before. Go to a gallery, a show, or a wrestling match. Whatever it is, the only requirement is that it be something that is out the ordinary for you.

Before we finish, let's look at a thought experiment. For this experiment let's divide our lives into three things: personal life, professional life, and emotional life.

Personal life we will define as physical and mental health. Do you think that your physical health would improve if you added even a little bit of the type of creative work that I have suggested? Do you think your cognitive powers would improve? All of the research says they will.

Professional life we will define as whatever it is that you do, and this could be wide ranging—you could be raising children, studying at school, or working in an office (or doing all three!). Do you think adding creativity will help in these areas? All of the research tells us it will.

Emotional life we will define as relationships with loved ones. As one simple example—do you think your romantic life would improve from some creativity? I'll leave you to ponder that one.

Your task: make a list of things you stopped doing because you are too busy. Bring one back for fifteen minutes a day. Plan some new events. Go to one.

# Plato

Draw an equilateral triangle sitting on its base. Write the name "Socrates" at the top. On the bottom corner at the left write "Plato." At bottom right, write "Aristotle." You are now looking at the most important formula for thought on our planet. These guys are the three stars of classical education.

In the old days, professors used to force every student to read these three stars. Do you know why? Because they knew what they were doing—everyone should read these three. It is just a good use of your time. The arguments attributed to these three form the bedrock of most of the debates that we are engaged in today. As such, if you read them, you can skip thousands of other authors and just focus on the source.

Sound too good to be true? It kind of is. We don't really know if Socrates existed in the way in which he had been reported, but that is really beside the point. What you need to know is that Socrates was a teacher, Plato was one of his students, and Aristotle was a student of both in turn. The real power of Socratic thinking shows up in the debate between Plato and Aristotle—in fact, it is so dramatic that many people divide themselves into camps, claiming they follow in one or the other tradition. Even more surprising is that you may be in one of those camps without knowing it.

Why does this matter to us?

The triangle.

Look at the triangle that you drew (or imagine it if you didn't actually draw it!). That triangle represents the *agora*. The agora was a place for the free exchange of ideas. It was the foundation of everything these three all-stars did. It was also a fierce place to learn. People spent their whole day debating over issues in every topic imaginable—politics, mathematics, astronomy, ethics, and aesthetics. All of these subjects matter to the study of creativity, but perhaps more than any other it is aesthetics that we need to check in with before going any further.

The simplest way to define aesthetics is, "the study of the beautiful." The one addition we need to make is that the notion of beauty here is something bigger than appearance and has to do with an overarching harmonious nature that is quite a bit more grand than what we think of today when we think of someone or something as beautiful. This type of philosophy is important to us because the kind of thinking that emerges from aesthetics is what lies at the heart of creative work. Think of it this way— when we engage in creative work, we are in pursuit of the beautiful.

So, why have a chapter on Plato and not one on Socrates?

Socrates did not record his teachings. Plato did; in fact he wrote most of his work as if Socrates was a character in a drama that Plato just happened to be writing down. That means that Plato is forever blurred into Socrates and vice versa.

So, why have a chapter on Plato in a book on creativity?

Boy, you sure are asking a lot of questions. The reason is that Plato is the first person to record a formalized study of aesthetics. Aristotle responds to it, and their discussion is the frame for all subsequent discussion about human creation and its place in the universe and in society.

So, can you give us a quick summary of all that I need to know about Plato's theory as it relates to creativity?

Of course I can, but first I need to make one quick note. Sometimes we will hear folks say that these three are the start of "Western" thought. That's incorrect. The theories contained in their work were spread across numerous societies and are discussed around the world. Forget the names and focus on the ideas—they are global.

Plato's thoughts on creativity in five simple steps:

1. Art is not as important as philosophical enquiry. Only philosophy can gain access to the truth and to beauty; creative endeavors are secondary at best. (This will be his biggest difference with Aristotle).

2. When it comes to art, you are what you eat. Therefore, if you take in a story that is too mushy, you will become mushy. (This argument is important because it launches the ideas of censorship and the control of information by those wishing to run society.)

3. For Plato, art is about copying, or what he calls *mimesis*—the replication of things that already exist. Since what you create is a copy it is worth less than the original. (This argument is important because it relates to our question about newness and also shows up in religious debate over representations of the sacred.)

4. Engaging with art will weaken your spirit by training you to accept false stories and false characters. (This argument is important for creativity because it accepts that what we work on directly impacts our health.)

5. Artists receive their inspiration from outside of themselves through a type of "divine inspiration," which they actually cannot properly transmit because they become the mouthpiece of the divine. Only some people will be able to translate what comes to them and thus, their work should not be widely distributed. (This argument is important because it deals with inspiration and the power of art, arguing that it is simply too much for the average person to deal with—it connects to the idea of censorship.)

These five elements form the heart of Plato's discussion of aesthetics. To these, he adds one other important consideration: *techné*. Techné refers to the use of the set of skills that a person brings to their work. Thus, a fine carpenter has techné. A doctor has techné. Unfortunately for the artist though, Plato does not feel that they have it. For Plato, artists divide their focus too broadly and as such are not really creating things that are of as much value as those that possess skills that they can use to contribute to society.

Here is an example of how this might work.

Say you are a storyteller and you write a story about a detective who chases criminals. In your story you write about the police and you write about a safe cracker who helps to rob banks. For Plato, because you are not actually a detective, all you are doing is copying the work of someone who actually has detective skills. Thus, the detective is capable of creating important work using skill, but the artist who writes about it is creating a copy that pales by comparison.

Now take this to the next step. If you are trying to organize a good society, it is not a good idea to have your citizens studying these false representations of detectives. Instead, they should learn about the genuine accomplishments of real detectives and the way in which they contribute to the betterment of society.

So, how do we connect this to our study of creativity?

Great question. Two ways. First, Plato would be all in favour of you trying to use creative measures to improve your work. The more that you find ways to enhance your participation in society the happier he would be. That sounds a little bit spooky, but he does not mean that he wants people to be drones; he wants them to be happy living in and working on the civilization of which they are a part.

The second involves the creative arts. In one of his most famous arguments, he seems to suggest that the ideal society would be best without artists who create work in the areas that we call the fine arts. People who, like Plato, but don't like his position on art, remind us that Plato actually wrote all of his philosophy in dramatic form; as dialogues. Another reason that is often given to explain his position is that Socrates—Plato's beloved teacher—was put to death by a society that Plato saw as corrupt. His views on controlling information and giving more status to philosophers like his teacher might be influenced by the time in which he lived.

You can make up your own mind about his position, but I would warn you against buying into his argument or dismissing it. In the end, what you want to do is to listen to the response created by Aristotle and then find your way into the debate. That response is what we will look at in the next chapter. In the meantime, I am going to give you one of the longer assignments of the book. Here we go:

Your task: Plato argues that art can be bad for your health. Write down three examples of art that you think might be bad for your health.

Please do not rush to do this assignment. Try to pick items that have been of major significance in your world. Think of popular music, film, books, video games, and any other area where work has been shared with large audiences. How might this work actually be bad for the people who experienced it? Plato believes that the rulers of society—for him, Philosopher Kings—should control what is shown to the population. Come up with one example of why this would be a good thing and one example of why it would be bad.

Aristotle

I am not certain if anyone would just happen to open the book and read this chapter first, but if you did, you should probably stop and read the previous chapter on Plato first, since most of what Aristotle does originates as a response to Plato.

In the last chapter, we looked at Plato's theory of the beautiful and his opinions on artists, art, and society's interest in controlling the messages that get to its citizens. Aristotle takes up Plato's argument and presents a counter-proposal that has become the most famous commentary on art in the world.

In *The Poetics*, Aristotle creates the first treatise on aesthetics. While Plato had some ideas presented in his works, it is Aristotle that puts together the first sustained study of the topic. He benefits from the groundwork laid by his predecessor, but he could not disagree with him more. We know that Aristotle wrote other works in this area, but unfortunately only *The Poetics* survives, and even that work is only preserved in a couple of manuscripts that were compiled from lost records in the medieval period.

In the work, Aristotle creates an anti-Platonic argument in order to launch his own theories on art and artists. The first thing you will need to know is that Aristotle is going to focus on what he calls "poetry." I put that in quotations because we need to think of poetry in a larger way than we currently do. For our discussion, think of it as creation from nothing done by artists or those wishing to create art. With that in mind, let's get to his argument.

Aristotle focuses on three questions:

1. What is poetry?

2. What kind of poetry is tragedy?

3. What are tragedy's essential elements?

He also discusses the role of the poet (remember, think about creators here, not just poets) in society. Plato argued that the ideal city should not have poets in it because they harm the people. Aristotle believed poets were important for society for three reasons:

1. The poet actually has knowledge that they are able to share;

2. The poet has a special ability to share universal truths with their fellow citizens;

3. The poet can provide virtuous, or good, education to the people.

In a famous quote that appears near the beginning of *The Poetics*, Aristotle lays out a response to Plato and introduces two important concepts that will be crucial to his argument. In the argument, he presents us with a study of tragedy. We do not have his writings on comedy, which are believed to have been lost.

Aristotle gives us a definition of his focal point. I will put the important terms in italics for you: "tragedy is the *mimesis* of a *serious* and complete *action* of some magnitude; in language embellished in various ways in its different parts; in dramatic, not narrative form; achieving, through pity and fear, the *catharsis* of such passions." Let's quickly look at those terms.

Mimesis is the word we got from Plato to describe the copying of something by the artist. Think of someone doing a painting of a sunset. The artist *mimes* or copies the sunset in paint on a canvas.

Serious is a qualitative word. Aristotle uses this to distinguish between mimesis that might be done purely for entertainment or distraction. True artists will do something that is qualitatively superior to this and thus of value for society. Deciding that value is a subject of a separate debate since it is difficult for us to agree on what is and is not of value and how much value any given work of art holds.

Action refers to more than just the activities of those represented. It has to do with the choices made by characters and how those choices connect to their character. It also extends to incorporate the way in which cause and effect operate in the world that is being replicated, copied, or presented by the artist.

Catharsis is perhaps the most talked-about word in all of Aristotle. It refers to the experience that occurs as we experience art. For Aristotle, the experience of art leads to a form of cleansing or transformational experience that he labels catharsis. Thus, in a story that involves the mimesis of serious and complete action, we the audience will experience a positive effect that cleanses us of parts of ourselves related to that work. It is then said to have had a "cathartic effect." It is important to note that catharsis is not fully dealt with in *The Poetics* but rather is fleshed out from other of Aristotle's works.

For Aristotle, these concerns often hinge on the representation of heroes. These heroes go through challenges or obstacles that cause them suffering and, in turn, arouses pity in the audience—though not so much as to cause them to suffer unduly—and shows us the experience of the fear of certain challenges and the ways in which it can be overcome. When the overall experience hits us, it cleanses us of the pity and fear through the process of catharsis. This cleansing effect is rather famous, but it is important to note that it should also be thought of as a kind of restorative—a move that returns balance to the individual citizen.

At the same time that audience members benefit from catharsis, there are also literal components that are of value. There is direct benefit from the study of the hero's experiences. How is the experience of this mimetic presentation of the events in a hero's life useful or important?

Aristotle's answer reveals the other side of the argument created by Plato. For Plato, the experience of the emotions involved in a story can weaken our constitution. For Aristotle, the experience of emotions through story can train us so that we are better prepared to face them in the real world. It can also introduce us to feelings that we may never have felt and might otherwise never feel but that can help us to make better decisions in our own lives.

Seeing art in this way, we need stories or artistic creations as part of our ongoing study of the way humans behave, and in particular, the way humans *should behave* if we are to be good citizens. Thus, for Aristotle, art is an essential component of our ongoing study of ethics, which is important for all mature people. As I am sure you can deduce, this means that the artist or creative person has a particularly important role to play in society.

Let's look more closely at some of the ideas Aristotle introduces. When discussing mimesis, Aristotle differs dramatically from Plato. For Aristotle, mimesis is something that is natural to human beings. He points out that when we are children we learn through mimicry, and he uses this example to demonstrate how essential it is to our education. For our work on creativity, this is particularly important. It shows us that the earliest studies of how we learn connect directly to creative work.

Aristotle extends his argument by saying that the mimesis of action—that is, the telling of stories or creation of expressive art—shows ideas that can be studied and learned from and not merely felt or experienced. Plato was concerned that the representation of emotions would weaken us. Aristotle points out that the emotions are not the primary concern of poetry or art—the events and experiences are the important components. These events form the basic parts of plot. For Aristotle, these moments are the big distinction. He felt that Plato spent too much time focused on characters and their emotions and not enough on the bigger picture.

Aristotle also dealt with *techné*. You will recall that Plato felt artists lack the ability to use of a set of specialized skills. For Aristotle, the skills of being an artist—the skills, for example, of the brush, pen, and body— are their own version of techné and can be learned, improved upon, and implemented in the performance of a useful practice.

Let's get back to our study of creativity.

The reason that Aristotle's response to Plato is so important is that it frames the debate over the importance of art and freedom of speech that continues to hold our attention today. Given that we are currently in what is supposed to be the *information age*, the discussion over whether or not to control what information citizens can hear is of utmost importance. Those working on creativity studies tend to come out in support of the free flow of ideas. Controlling information reduces the input that can fuel creative work. That said, we must not lose sight of Plato's argument that what we consume can have a direct impact on our emotional, physical, and psychological health. The debate continues and will not, and cannot, be resolved.

Your task: list three stories or artistic creations that you feel give examples that help people to live more positive lives. The stories themselves do not have to be positive, they just have to offer the potential of learning a lesson that can be of use in our day-to-day lives.

Aesthetics 12

In the last two chapters we looked at the ways in which Plato and Aristotle began a discussion of aesthetics. Aesthetics, we said, is the study of the beautiful, but in such a way that "beautiful" means something larger than personal attraction or pleasing appearance—here we might think of the latter as merely "pretty."

Why does this matter for our study of creativity? There are a lot of reasons, but the central one involves the fact that aesthetics introduces the concept of the evaluation, critique, or weighting of art. Now, there are two outcomes from this—one leads us into a discussion of the nature of art and how it might be evaluated and discussed by a variety of people; the other uncovers the challenges that can arise when we allow critical evaluation to shut down our ability to experiment with our own creativity.

In order to move forward we need to have a brief discussion of how we can talk about creativity. The majority of these debates start by reflecting on things like poetry, painting, sculpture, dance, theatre, and the like, but as you know we want to use the same elements to analyze *all* creative practice. So, let's proceed with a simple example.

Let's assume that you are a painter. You decide that you are going to do a picture of your mom. You finish your painting and it gets put in a gallery downtown. I show up, and I am expected to write a review of your work for the local arts magazine and post an evaluation online. What am I going to talk about?

Right away, we confront the question: "what is art"? Or perhaps more clearly, "what is the nature of art"? We can think of this question as "what is the x-ness of x"? That is, what is it about art that makes it art? Once we have a way of talking about a creative piece we can evaluate its successes and failures and produce a commentary that may be of use to our fellow citizens.

So, for the sake of our example, let's set up a thought experiment. If you had to do a painting of your mother and try to capture more than just a photo—to really get at who she is to you, to herself, and to others—how would you proceed to paint? Don't spend too much time on this, but please realize that you have some choices about how you would move forward.

Now imagine your picture of your mother.

I, as the critic, come along and look at your painting. What kinds of things can I talk about? What *paint-liness* aspects of this work can I evaluate? I might look at the choice of medium—watercolor, oils, or mixed media—and talk about whether you made it work, whether you show facility with the medium. I might look in more detail at the brush strokes or the use of color and shadowing. I might look at what this painting tells me about your mother. Given that I don't know her, the message that this painting sends arrives on a blank slate, right? Or does it?

Of course it doesn't. One of the important considerations for us to remember is that my preferences come into play, as does my psychology. The idea of a painting that portrays a "mother" might cause me to bring up feelings about my own mother or of the stereotypes of motherhood.

But if this is the case, and all I am doing is having my own personal experience, how can I possibly hope to comment on the painting?

Expertise.

Take a moment and consider the selection of a medium and the example of brush strokes. If you are able to demonstrate real prowess in those areas, I can evaluate—or attempt to evaluate—your techné. You will recall from the debate between Plato and Aristotle in the last two chapters that techné is the use of advanced skills in the production of something of value.

But, let's extend this further—or rather, let me make a suggestion and allow you to make up your mind. I come along as the critic to evaluate your painting and its brushstrokes. You worry that all I will do is use my own personal, subjective, taste to evaluate the piece, which means that your work gets evaluated in a way that is really little more than random chance. If I like it, you win; if I don't, you lose. Critics, however, argue that they, like artists, have techné. Their evaluative and communicative skills are their stock and trade. As such, they should—following this example—be able to show up and render a professional opinion of your work regardless of the personal taste and baggage that they bring to the work.

The big question here is: do you think critics have techné? Scholars have had this debate for years. Some of the arguments go like this: can someone teach poetry if they don't actually write poetry themselves? Most people in the academy believe that criticism and teaching have their own techné so that you do not necessarily have to practice an art in order to teach it. You should make up your own mind on this, but I will give you my take. In my experience, there are a lot of accomplished artists who cannot teach their art. There are also a lot of accomplished teachers who do not practice the art they critique. There are also some folks that land in between and can do both. In the end, it comes down to the individual.

So, let's get back to your painting example. We have established that one way of conducting evaluation is to attempt to assess the techné. That can mean the brushstrokes, but it could also mean the way in which you use your culture. What does that mean? Here's an example: say you live in a world that celebrates large families and you paint your mother holding many babies and she is glowing, or you paint her holding one child and looking dejected. In this case, Aristotle would say you are using your techné to examine a universal truth.

Finally, let's imagine that I come to the gallery and I evaluate your painting, and I say that you are the greatest painter of your generation. The story begins to spread, the value of your work on the market goes up, and now people want to buy the painting as well as your earlier works. Museums and galleries now want to have some of your work because it is their job to portray the best works available and you've been deemed a great painter.

The next thing you know, students in high school, college, and university have to study your work in order to be considered educated. They sit in a classroom and someone shows a slide of your painting of your mother and tells the class that you are the greatest painter of your generation and that this painting is the piece that launched your career. See any problems here?

We run into problems when someone in one of those classrooms says, "but why should I like this painting?" If the students have a bad teacher, that person might be ridiculed as having an inferior palate—that is, they are too stupid to appreciate your great painting of your mother. But, what if that person is smarter than the original critic and sees through your painting in a way that I could not when I did the evaluation that launched your career? That's where all the fun begins.

Let's try and summarize what's at stake here. Over the past number of years certain people have pointed out that we all have different taste and, as such, we cannot really talk about the qualities of any given painting in an objective way. On the other hand, people argue that surely we can distinguish the difference in techné demonstrated by my finger painting of my grouchy boss and Michelangelo's painting of the Sistine Chapel. Both groups are right, and both provide us with one idea that is crucial to our study of creativity.

The first point is that all judgment is relative. That's good news for us because one of the biggest obstacles to people pursuing their own creative work is judgment. If you stop painting because someone tells you that you are no good you are losing an incredible amount, and they are harming you in a way that is just plain wrong. Even more important is the fact that after we hear critics all our lives we begin to internalize those voices and judge everything we do harshly on our own. One of the most devastating things that I encounter when working with students is that they are far too hard on themselves, and it stops them from really doing their best work. Try to get past this type of judgment—it will change your life.

The second group teaches us that there are good critics out there who have their own techné. In a world that is overwhelmed with information, these experts can help save you time by drawing your attention to work that you might want to consider. They can also help advanced creators get better at their craft. Just remember that no one is perfect, and you are free to profit from their advice or to ignore it.

Your task: think back to a time that someone criticized your work quite strongly. Try to remember how that felt. Record how that critique impacted the way you work.

Theatre

For the next several chapters we are going to look at specific areas of creative expression. We will start with the fundamentals and work our way to the exciting new world of blended or multimedia arts. To really understand just how fascinating our current situation is, it is best to ground ourselves in all of the disciplines that are now contributing to the rich world of creativity we work in today.

Theatre lies at the heart of every civilization on earth. From the start of time we have enacted scenes from life for one another in order to share our experience of this world. As Aristotle first pointed out, as creatures we are naturally drawn to mimicry as a way to teach one another and to explore the issues of our lives. The stories we tell can be as varied as how to hunt, how to run, the challenges of a hero's quest, or important moments in a war or other conflict. At the heart of every civilization, theatre provides us with a proving ground for our ideas.

Perhaps the most important lesson that you can ever learn about theatre is that it is human research. What does that mean? Have you ever heard of the use of animals to test certain products and drugs? It's quite a controversial area in our society. It gets even more controversial when we want to test things on humans. In fact, it is almost impossible to test on humans for reasons that I am sure you can imagine. But consider this, theatre is in fact a practice that allows us to do research on humans.

Think of it this way. You go to see a play. The premise of the play is that a young man commits a murder and thinks he can get away with it. There is no evidence connecting him to the murder, but his conscience begins to trouble him and his own actions lead to his arrest and conviction for the crime. In this fashion, the playwright and the team that put on the production of the show are conducting an experiment in human behavior from which the audience can learn. Make sense?

Now for a quick word about theatre in relation to film and video games. Theatre involves live performance. The difference between live and recorded is quite important. For our purposes, we want to experience both, but we need to be clear about why live performance needs to be part of your creative diet.

Let's turn to a thought experiment. Have you ever been with a friend or family member when they went through something really tough? Something like a relationship breakup, the loss of a job, or the death of a loved one? Do you remember how you felt? Of course, your mind was working away and assessing the situation and causing you to think sympathetically, but another very real experience occurs in your body. We now know that the reason for this reaction is that our systems are wired to experience empathetic connections with people we are physically near.

So, here's a challenge for you. Find a live performance to go to and test out the theory I just mentioned. Two warnings though: first, you have to allow yourself to feel it. What the heck does that mean? Well, think again of the example of the experience with your loved one. They were suffering and you cared about them, so you were *there* being sympathetic. Now imagine that you didn't care about them—that you hated them or distrusted them in some way. Then while they were sharing their experience you could just cross your arms and refuse to be moved by their pain.

If you go to a show, you have to allow yourself to feel the performance. If you do so, it will impact you in a whole different way because your neurons will be allowed to react in the way they were designed to operate. The second warning you can't do much about—if the performers are not really *present* in performance, there won't be anything for you to feel in the first place other than, perhaps, their nervousness at being on stage.

Okay, let's get to some things about theatre that you may not know. First, theatres are often used as models for students studying in business schools. The reason? Theatrical productions have to deliver on time and must always produce a product. Ever heard of the phrase "the show must go on"? That refers to the fact that theatre people must always be on time and can never miss work. There are a few notable exceptions, but you will notice that when people don't live up to that commitment to produce a show on time, people will make noise about it.

The next thing you should know is that theatre is about as multidisciplinary as you can get. If you are interested in working on an art project with other people, theatre is a great place to get involved. Let me give you an example.

A few years ago I was in a production of the Shakespeare play *A Midsummer Night's Dream*. For this production, our creative team included actors, a director, a musical director, musicians, a choreographer, dancers, carpenters, electricians, a lighting designer, a costume designer, a set designer, seamstresses and builders, welders who made a metal tree that a dozen actors could climb on, stage managers to organize us, dramaturges who helped with the script, and operators for the sound, lights, and running of the show. All in all it was dozens of people all working together on a project.

The lesson in this has to do with the nature of creativity. The project was one that was based on creative work. If we did our job well, the audience would be able to experience a play that asks questions about the nature of love between couples. In order to do that, though, we were all able to exercise our creative muscles. For example, our welders were incredibly talented at their jobs—that is, they had *techné* as welders. That said, I'll bet you that they had never been asked to create a two-and-a-half story tree before. That's a creative challenge. It was the same with everyone on the project; we benefited from the collective, creative endeavor of putting on a show.

Of course, it's easy to see how a show is a creative experience, but you need to recognize that this can be a model for any type of collective work. What we did was put a group of highly skilled people in a room and give them a challenge to do something they had never done before and to do it on time and on budget. And you know what? They did it. And they had fun. Now, I know you can see how that might be a useful example.

So far, though, we have only described the experience of those making the show. There are two fundamental components in theatre. The one we've just described is the person or persons who wish to share a certain message or experience in space and in real time. The second, and most important component, is the audience. Have you ever heard an actor get an award and thank the audience? They are doing that for a reason. In live performance the audience plays an *active* and vitally necessary role.

Here's the simplest way I can explain this role. Have you ever had a conversation with someone who just doesn't get what you are saying? Say you are trying to tell a joke and they just give you a blank stare, or you are trying to explain something amazing that happened to you and they just sit there. Do you notice what that does to your ability to communicate?

It kind of kills it. The reason is that they are being a lousy audience (or you are an awful storyteller, but I'm giving you the benefit of the doubt!). Now imagine that on a large scale. If you are telling a story to an *active* audience that is leaning forward, listening to your every word, and reacting to what you say in the moment, it is an incredible experience. The theatre needs that audience. Go ask anyone who works in theatre and they will tell you the audience is the most important thing. As an audience member you have the power to make the performance soar, or you can pin it to the ground and kill it.

So, what should you watch for when you go to theatre? Everything. Look for acting, costume, movement, sound, light, set, overall storytelling, the execution of the various technical components, and audience engagement. It is perhaps the most dynamic art form ever devised, and if it is done right you will feel it. That means that if you go and you give it your *active* attention and it does not work then those folks are not doing their job. You are the audience member and as long as you show up and participate you are holding up your end of the deal; the rest is up to those bringing you the show. That means that if it is a Shakespeare play, they should make it make sense to you. If they are doing something experimental, maybe it won't make sense in the traditional sense, but it should touch you or engage you on some physical level or they have failed in their undertaking.

One of the most famous directors ever to work in theatre thought of it this way: going to a bad movie can still be enjoyable because there are lots of flashing lights (and popcorn!), but going to bad theatre is physically painful. The reason? If you are there and actively participating you will actually feel what is happening. Theatre requires something from you rather than just passively laying back and taking everything in. It means that going to a live performance can be demanding, so make sure you are in the right mood to go.

Your task: go to a play and try to be an active audience member. As soon as you can after the show, record your impressions both mentally and physically.

Visual Arts

Visual arts have a particularly important role to play in the study of creativity in our time. For years, we have been quite good at teaching students to be literate. We teach reading and writing and test reading comprehension at all levels at school. We have not been as good at training people for visual comprehension. We are getting a lot better at it, but we still have a long way to go, particularly given that so much of our daily information is coming to us through visual media.

The journey of the visual image is a long one. From cave paintings to computer-generated landscapes, human beings have been enamored with visual representation. Many educational theorists now believe that half of the population is made up of visual as opposed to textual learners. These people apparently have a more complex relation to visual images than those who are book readers.

The evaluation of visual work started with carvings and cave paintings. In the case of the latter, found in various parts of the world, the creators seem to have been leaving messages related to their lives and their beliefs. Images of actual animals but also symbols made up of parts of fictitious beings seem to imply that humanity's desire to express itself through the image is long standing.

Our first true critiques of visual art focus on painting. In its earliest stages, commentary focused on mimesis or what art critics call representation. In this case, works of art were judged for their ability to capture a realistic portrayal of their subject. Many people still feel that this is the most important value of visual arts; however, the way we look at accurate representation has changed since painters began experimenting with abstraction and since the invention of photographic equipment.

So, let's look at how we might evaluate work that we encounter in the visual world. The first way we can go about something is to do what we call a formal analysis. Formal analysis would involve things like an examination of line, colour, texture, light, and so on. You would evaluate the artist's facility with these things and perhaps even take a stab at the impact of these elements on the viewer.

Now, you can probably tell that this way of doing an evaluation of the work seems to be focused very much on the craft side of the painting. It works for us because it connects to what Aristotle talked about when he discussed an artist's *techné,* but it falls a little flat when dealing with the engagement of the person experiencing the work.

To counter the shortcomings of a purely formal approach we can talk about the experience of the work. It turns out that this particular area is quite controversial, but it really does not need to be. We are actually hard wired to appreciate or evaluate art with our bodies, but sometimes we don't pay attention. Let's do a thought experiment.

Picture yourself in a white room. The lighting is bright but not so bright that it hurts your eyes. Picture someone entering the room and asking you to close your eyes. She has a painting in her hands that is covered by a blanket. She hangs the picture and removes the blanket. It has a picture of a landscape that is the most beautiful place you have ever seen—in fact, it looks just like your dream home. The detail is incredible—the painting almost seems alive. How do you feel? What would you comment on?

Okay, erase that image. Now the woman hangs the picture and removes the cover and the painting is covered in softly colored shapes of various colors. How would this make you feel? What might you comment on?

Finally, imagine she removes the blanket and there are shapes that seem to remind you of something. Maybe even body parts. There are very bright colors that seem to almost have been thrown at the painting and they do not seem to go with one another. How do you feel? What might you comment on?

Now, this is a very simple exercise, but what I hope you get out of it is that we all have a lot of things that we can talk about when it comes to visual art. The problem is that we are often too shy to admit it for fear of being told that we do not know what we are talking about. I often have students look at various images and sometimes people will say that they don't understand something, but why should we have to understand something? The creative drive is all about trying to engage things that mystify us. Taking a look at a series of paintings that confuse the heck out of you can really help to shake up your thinking and feeling.

All of this is a diluted way of looking at engaging with visual art, but we have to start somewhere. Each day you are flooded with visual messages that are being put in front of your eyes by experts that are trying to cause you to have a reaction. Wouldn't it be nice to be a little more aware of what is going on with visual communication?

Let's go back to our painting. Let's work with that first one—the one that shows you a version of your dream home (or place) that somehow seems more alive than a photograph or traditional painting. There are two ways you can talk about it—you can try to look at the technique and assess how the painter used their *techné* to create this work, or you can talk about the experience you have that comes about as the result of seeing a painting of your dream home.

The real realm of actively engaging with the painting requires us to comment on both of these arenas—the mimetic quality and the experiential component of encountering the work. I say "encounter" because it is a very different experience to look at a painting by Van Gogh online or in a book compared with actually seeing one of his paintings in a gallery. There is something different to be gained by seeing and being in close proximity with the work.

Once you begin to actually pay attention to visual art, you will notice that some artists emphasize one element more than others and that you have to take that difference into account when and if you want evaluate the work. There will always be a subjective element to the work, but do your best not to be dismissive if you encounter something that does not "make sense." It may well be that art that does not make sense is just what you need to expand your visual thinking.

One quick note before we move on to an examination of visual culture in your day-to-day life. The advent of photography created a seismic shift in work in the visual realm. You can use many of the same types of criteria for evaluating photographs that you do for painting. Obviously there are some new items to consider: the framing, the use of various film stocks, formats, manners of manipulation, and now digital components to the process. Perhaps the most important note for us as good, creative thinkers is that we should remember that photographs do not necessarily show the "truth."

Since the inception of photography, people have seen pictures as a means of seeing the truth of an event. The trouble is that the photographer has a great deal of leeway that allows her to manipulate what the photo shows. And that was before the development of digital photography and various software packages that allow for detailed manipulation of the image first captured.

For us, there are some very interesting new debates that arise because of the way in which photography engages with mimesis. Think of a famous painting that you have seen. Think of what its value might be at auction. Now consider how many copies have been made and sold in gallery shops and shopping malls. What does this do to our evaluation of creativity as something new that has value?

Finally, let's take a look at how visual art connects to your life. How do you express yourself visually? Do you have a selection of photos that are important to you? Do you share them online? Why those photos? Do you have pictures by others that you like? Dislike? Why? Do you spend a lot of time on how your hair looks? Your clothing? Your car? Your home? Do you draw or doodle? Is there a certain spot that you like to go because of its appearance? Are there business logos that you like? Some that turn you off? Do you have a favorite colour?

You live in a world that is sending you more and more visual images. In the past, we got most of our information through text. When that was the case, we trained everyone in reading and writing so that they would understand the messages and be able to make up their own minds. Have you been trained to evaluate the messages that people are sending with logos, advertising campaigns, or important reports involving graphs, pictures, and renderings?

We express ourselves visually and we are soaked in visual images each day, yet we receive very little training in how this form of communication works.

Your task: write down three ways you communicate visually.

Plastic Arts

The "plastic arts" can be a bit of a misleading title. It refers to solid objects that exist in space. The earliest art form that we can think of under this category is sculpture. In much the same way as our discussion of painting in the last chapter, a discussion of sculpture will provide us with information that is of use when we discuss other developments in plastic arts. These might include the design and building of skyscrapers and bridges, the construction of cars, or the creation of pieces of installation art. Even *haute couture* is a form of plastic art.

Sculpture is one of the world's oldest art forms, but it can come in for some pretty harsh criticism. Scholars tell us that the reason people don't take sculpture as seriously as painting is that most of us experience sculpture in public. Very often big buildings or parks will contain sculptures, and we see them as part of our daily walks. Birds sit on them and leave behind messages that cannot possibly help the value of the work.

The real problem, however, is an old bias that pervades the way we look at the plastic arts. For a long time now we have thought of things that involve the body as somehow of lesser importance than things that involve the mind. Thus, sitting and reading a poem or painting a water-color is somehow more valuable because it seems to connect to our minds more than to our bodies. Educators often point out that, as a result of this bias, people who are not very creative tend to think of music as superior to dance. The reason is that you can sit quietly and listen to music and use only your head, while dance directly involves the body, about which we tend to be too embarrassed to talk.

Of course, that is all changing now as the world gets more connected and as we drop old ideas that were deeply flawed. But, let's get back to sculpture.

When we want to approach sculpture in order to evaluate it, one thing jumps out immediately. Sculpture exists in three dimensions in space. Thus, if you go to a gallery to look at a painting that is hanging on the wall, you cannot walk around back of the painting. You can walk around the sculpture and examine it as an object in space. This special set of characteristics is incredibly important. It turns out that our bodies can feel other bodies in space. Just think of that feeling you get when some-one walks up behind you; you can feel them there. Sculpture speaks to us through our bodies and our minds. You can also walk up to a sculpture and feel it. Touching the sculpture allows you to evaluate how the sculp-tor went about creating the work in front of you.

Taken another step, our experience with sculpture brings us back to ourselves. We lead our lives as moving containers. In whatever way you conceive of yourself, you are connected to a three-dimensional body that occupies space. As such, sculpture provides us with experimentation that has direct relevance for our experience in the world. You don't need to overthink this idea; your body can experience it for itself.

Want some examples?

Have you ever been in a room that made you uncomfortable? Why did it make you feel that way? Have you ever been to a large event—say a sporting event or a concert? How did you feel being in the space with all those other bodies? Did that feeling change your experience of the event? Have you ever visited someone's home and been struck by how the home reflected their personality? Do you decorate your room with things that help to explain who you are?

People who successfully manipulate space work in a variety of different fields. Studies of athletes who play sports like soccer, hockey, and football turn up stories of people who can feel space moving in very particular ways. In some cases, peak-performance athletes describe the ability to sense space in 360 degrees around them as they move through it.

Members of the military and law enforcement are likewise trained to pay special attention to space and the movement of bodies and objects through it. Boxers and martial artists become experts at the three dimensional body and its functions in space.

But what does this have to do with the average person who wants to work on their creativity?

We all live in space, and we all interact with people and objects in that space. Learning to communicate or to understand objects in three dimensions will improve your ability to engage with people and places. Thus, the study of sculpture helps us to begin to develop a tool kit for understanding the world in which we live—both inside and outside of our bodies.

Perhaps more important than the direct learning of spatial knowledge is the opportunity to learn in a different way. If you are already a spatial learner, you are probably getting plenty of opportunities to expand your textual knowledge in school or at work. If, on the other hand, you are a classic textual/arithmetical thinker, taking some time to engage with the world of objects in space can offer you a very dramatic way to stretch your thinking capabilities.

So, how are you going to begin to develop those skills? Well, for the purposes of this chapter, we need to make a distinction. It turns out that spatial skills play a huge role in the world of computer games and contemporary film. We'll talk about those items in later chapters, but for the time being trust me when I tell you that working on your skills understanding objects in space can help improve the way you engage with games and film but also with more abstract things like databases and webs of information.

Where will you find sculpture in your city? In art schools, galleries, and public spaces. Go and take a look. Stand there for a bit. Move around the piece. Try and gauge the formal components—size, texture, colour, materials, placement, etc. At the same time, see if you can take account of how it feels. We often find that objects with lots of smooth surfaces and curves make us feel calm, while more angular pieces put us on guard. Does that happen for you?

Now let's take it in the opposite direction. Let's experience some space. The next time you are outdoors do the same exercise. What are the limits to the space? Are there skyscrapers all around you? Are you fenced in on one or more sides? See if you can't describe the nature of the space. How does it sound? Is it loud? Does some surface bounce or eat sound causing the experience to change? And, again, evaluate how this space makes you feel. I love big, open spaces—they just make me feel more energized than being closed in. Some people really hate being closed in—is that you? Some prefer it. What is it about space that causes people to react the way they do?

Now try some architectural spaces. Pick one or two rooms that have a particular effect on you. What's a good room look like for you? What does it feel like? Write down a few items that come to mind. How does a big room with a high ceiling make you feel when compared with a small room with a low ceiling? A light or dark room?

Finally, take a look at major traffic spaces. I am not talking cars here, but walking traffic. Do you have places that you have to walk through on a regular basis that have a lot of other people in them? What does it feel like when it is really crowded? Have you ever walked there at a time when there were fewer people? Did that feel different? If you had to go for a walk, what type of walkway would you choose?

The final component of our spatial self-test is personal space. Have you ever had someone stand so close to you that it felt uncomfortable? How far away would you have preferred that they stand? Alternately, have you ever tried to talk to someone that was so skittish they kept moving away? How close did you want to get in order to feel that you were communicating? If you were to imagine sitting down right now in the most comfortable spot imaginable, what would that space be like? How close would the nearest person be?

Why so many questions?

Because we really need to make sure that we spend some time on primary spatial recognition. You will notice that a lot of these questions will have answers that come down to personal preference. That is absolutely fine. The practice of paying attention to our spatial life is what we are really after. Some people are naturally good at this, but many of us are not, and we spend very little time in our schools discussing these issues. If you do not pay attention to space you can cost yourself a lot of comfort, productivity, and ultimately, creativity.

The final thing you need to pay attention to in our spatial exercises is tactility. That means touch. It's the simplest, but in many ways the most complex, of our engagements with the plastic arts. That's because when we see things with certain textures our brains fire off messages as if we were touching those things. Are there certain things that you like the feel of? Are there some you do not like at all?

Your task: write down and keep your answers to the earlier questions.

Music

When asked, almost everyone says they love music. After that, the similarities end. For whatever reason, musical taste seems to be one of the areas where almost everyone has a strong opinion. For years, I worked as a musician and since then I've spent years working on projects that involve music. If there is any one lesson that I have learned, it is that if you have any desire to be creative you need to let go of your biases around taste.

Perhaps you don't have this problem—and you are fortunate if you don't—but many people I know have a list of performers or bands that they absolutely love to hate. Not only that, but they can give you a speech about why these folks are no good at the drop of a hat. That's a heck of a lot of energy to expend on something you don't like. As I mentioned earlier in the book, the more you delve into creative work, the more you begin to appreciate that everyone has something positive to contribute and that judgment is the arch enemy of creativity. It's a use of energy that would be better placed elsewhere.

Stranger still are the small group of music "fans" who will stop liking a particular performer if others begin to like them. So caught up in the mystique of owning their particular taste are these folks that they will actually say, "oh, I liked them before everyone else did." So what? Seriously, did the song change once your neighbor bought the track and started playing it on infinite loop?

Why is it that music evokes such a strong response in people? I want to borrow a rather complicated sounding phrase from a famous author. Drawing on inspiration from our good friend Aristotle, the Irish author James Joyce spoke of the "ineluctable modality of the visible." What he meant was that we have no control over the input that enters through our eyes and into our brains. I've always loved that phrase, but I've also always thought that it made even more sense when it comes to sound. Rephrased then, it would be the "ineluctable modality of the aural."

Let's look at two examples of this type of effect, one positive and one negative. Have you ever been somewhere and heard a song that you liked that immediately cheered you up or energized you? Chances are you have. So common is this effect that it's been used in multiple movies and television programs as a means of entertainment.

Now let's look at the opposite. Have you ever been at a party or other function where the music was simply awful? How did that affect your interpretation of the event? For many of us, bad music can be so powerful that we will do anything we can to find our way to the door, even if the event would otherwise be attractive to us.

Filmmakers, producers of plays, and astute hosts of events know that music has this kind of power, and they use it to help get their message across. Strings kick in when we are supposed to be feeling the love in a romantic scene, pulsing music announces suspense, and swirling sounds deliver the culmination of important scenes. Owners of shops send messages to their customers about what type of people are their target customers by the musical selection they play.

For the purposes of our work, we need to find a way to talk about music in a slightly more formal way. We won't talk about musical notation, though it is worth mentioning in passing that we now have multiple studies that tell us that practicing music formally will improve your mental function throughout your life. For us, however, all we want to do in this chapter is find a way to discuss music immediately so that we can reap the benefits in terms of our broader creative practice.

There are a number of ways that we can talk about music. The first is called *expressionist*. This method basically refers to the feeling that is attached to music. We all know what a sad song sounds like, and we all know what a happy song sounds like. What we want to do in order to get better at this is to get a little bit more nuanced in the way we can talk about the type of reaction we get from a piece of music. A simple way to begin to stretch your musical vocabulary is to pick two sad songs and try and write down in a few words how their sadness is different.

Another way that is often used is the connective communication approach. In this mode, we look at music in terms of messages that it sends that connect to some external truth or lesson. People often talk about Beethoven's *Ode to Joy* when they bring up this type of appreciation. The trick here is that you don't want to get too literal. That means, that if a singer sings the phrase "do unto others as you would have them do unto you" it is not the music that is sending you that message if all you are doing is taking those words at face value. There is a difference between a narrow, literal interpretation and a more fully creative one. If we stick to our *Ode to Joy* example, we might hear the song sung in another language, yet we still seem to get a lofty, celebratory message.

As with all art forms, there is also the formalist way of analyzing music. Formalist means analyzing each of the parts that go into building the piece and how they work together. Highly trained musicians can speak about elements of music that are beyond the scope of this book, but even for those who have never studied music, we should be able to do a simple analysis of why the different parts that we hear are present and how they work along with the rest of the elements of the song.

When we think of parts of a song there are a number of ways to go about breaking a piece of music down. You can look at overall parts, such as beginning, middle, and end. You can search for repetitions or parts of the music that seem to respond to one another or develop on something that came before. You can also break down the instruments into sections or individual lines so that you can appreciate what is being contributed. Try to take into account the timing or the pace of the different parts of the piece to which you are listening. Add to that an attention to the varia-tions in intensity (think louder and quieter or harder and softer) that are present in the song. Finally, pay attention to the silences. All musicians use silence as one of their tools.

One important question that a lot of people bring up has to do with representation. You will recall that Aristotle talked about mimesis, or the reproduction of something from real life. Critics often ask if music can really be a mimetic art. That is, can music actually copy something from real life and express it to an audience, or is its communication solely through emotion and cognitive lines that have to be established through the study of the form?

Put more simply, think of an event in your life. Something impor-tant. Do you think it would be possible to write a song that would express it? And before you say yes, remember that you can't just be a literalist and write lyrics that tell the story straight out. It's a complicated question, and people disagree over the answer. It doesn't matter what your answer is, but you should have an opinion that you can explain.

So, why bother going to all this trouble if we all—or almost all—already love music? Actually, the answer is in the question. Due to the strength of the influence of music on us, we have to go that extra mile in order to analyze how it works if we hope to expand our ability to appreciate music as part of our creative development. It is the things that we take for granted that we have to spend the most time on if we are to free our minds up for more creative thinking.

There are two major things that you can do to help yourself work on creativity. The first and most obvious is to try and take up an instrument if you can. Forget about whether you are good or not—the benefits from studying music have been demonstrated in multiple studies and the results are extraordinary. People who study are actually able to use parts of their brains that others simply cannot access. If you are too busy or you don't feel comfortable, pick something simple. It only takes a little bit of effort to start the process. Even five minutes a day can help.

The second task is somewhat easier. Start listening to music and asking the questions listed previously discussed. Once you get a little bit better at analyzing the music you are listening to, it is time to start listening to music that is new. Start out slowly, but see if you can start listening to music from different cultures and different styles than you normally listen to at home. Be ready for this to be a bit challenging. Different cultures use different musical scales and rhythm patterns, and hearing things that we are not used to can be jarring at first.

Remember, though, if it sounds strange and makes you start to feel a little bit different that's a good sign! It means you are out of your comfort zone and on a bit of a musical adventure.

Your task: learn how to play a new musical instrument. Okay, just kidding, but it sure would be great if you could. Instead, try listening to a familiar piece of music and writing down some of the things I mentioned. Do the same with a new piece of music.

Dance

Dance holds a special place in the study of creativity for a couple of important reasons. The first is that it is the central example used by Sir Ken Robinson in his now famous TED talk focusing on creativity and education. The second is that recent discoveries in neuroscience have taught us that our old ideas of a separate mind and body are deeply misplaced.

A lesser reason that dance is particularly important in this book is that, for me, it is the only one of the fine arts in which I have not personally worked. I have had to learn dances for plays, but no one would ever mistake me for a dancer. Strangely, though, it is for this reason that dance has been so important in my own work. Several years ago when I began my research into creativity and performance, I realized that I would need to study dance in order to speak coherently about it as a subject but also in order to speak about creativity as a whole. Over the past few years, I have travelled to numerous cities to see dance; I've studied dance film and books about dance, and I still find myself excited by what I do not understand about it.

My curiosity about dance connects to one of the central rules about creativity—you must explore things that you do not understand. My passion for dance comes, at least partly, from the fact that it is the area of the fine arts that I understand the least. Interestingly, though, I can be deeply impacted by a great dance show. While this is only anecdotal evidence, it is a kind of proof of the idea that we do not need to understand the formal terms of a given form of artistic expression in order to connect to the performance.

But enough about me, let's get back to Ken Robinson.

In 2006, Robinson gave a talk whose title asked "Do Schools Kill Creativity?" The central example that he used was the dancer Gillian Lynne. As a child, Lynne was thought to have a learning disability until a psychologist told her parents that there was nothing wrong with her. He explained that she was a born dancer. Enrolling her in dance classes immediately changed her performance in school, and Lynne went on to become one of the most successful dancers and choreographers in the world.

I am a strange advocate for dance, but in many ways I think it is one of the most important things you can explore. The reason for this ties in to all of the points I have listed. First, as Robinson says, we do not pay enough attention to work that involves the body. Second, as neuroscience tells us, separating our minds from our bodies is a mistake. We need to move to thrive, and moving improves not only health and dexterity, it improves cognition. Third, even if you are like me and you are a little too stupid to understand just what the heck they are doing up there, your body understands. We respond to what the dancers, choreographers, and their collaborators bring before us.

So, let's take a look at some of the things we might want to look for when we go to see a dance piece. Before we do that, though, we need to clear up something that comes up every time I teach this section to my creativity class.

There are a lot of different kinds of dance. All cultures have dances, and dance has been a part of human expression since earliest times. People who study dance and consider dance their primary focus have a complex range of skills they can bring to the world of physical expression. Often, these people who work all day every day at the art form become frustrated when the public thinks of dance as the type of stuff that is run on contests, shows, or in bars. That is understandable. At the same time however, it is important to let anyone who wants to dance do so. Sometimes these popular expressions can help draw more people in to the more advanced work of serious dance professionals. This brings us to a challenge. When you start to explore dance, try to make sure that you not only get a sampling of diverse styles from multiple cultures but also add trips to professional dance companies or schools that are developing new work. These folks are the ones on the front lines, and they are the ones that will test your assumptions about the body, movement, and dance and will give you the best opportunity to expand your creative abilities.

While dance is as old as human experience, the formal study of it is relatively new. When we come to think of dance, we can start by drawing comparisons with other art forms. Certainly dance shares much with theatre and music. It is, or at least it has been, an art form designed for a live audience. It is also often connected to organized sound or music that runs in collaboration with the movement. Costuming, makeup, and lighting are also integral components of the form. Remember, if the dancer decides to use no lights, costume, or makeup that, too, is a choice.

The key point is that with dance, and dance alone, the physical realm is of highest importance.

In Ken Robinson's famous talk he discusses an issue that many others have also examined. Within the fine arts there seems to be a hierarchy that places dance at the bottom and music and art at the top. The explanation that is given is that dance involves the body and wherever we find an art form that privileges the body over the mind we think of it as being a lesser form.

Science is now telling us what dancers have known for years—that the mind and the body are not separate at all. At the same time, dance is growing rapidly in its popularity among those interested in the creative arts. It is also growing among those interested in finding better ways to teach children. The more we learn about ourselves, the more sense dance makes.

Here we must pause to examine new technology. In my experience, few art forms have benefited as much from new technology as dance. For years, it has been difficult to increase audiences and to reach those who might not otherwise see the ongoing explorations of the art of the body in motion. With digital technology, all of this has changed. We are now able to find examples of multiple kinds of forms instantaneously. In another exciting development, virtual reality has provided those who might not be able to dance in this world with the opportunity to explore the form in another. As always, I will remind you that to truly experience some dance there is no substitute for being there, but in the case of many forms the digital experience is a wonderful substitute, and in some cases has become the primary means of expression.

Dance is a multifaceted art. When you see a performance you might well ask yourself the famous question, can I separate the dancer from the dance? Is the dance the motion of the body or bodies, or is it the resulting shapes in relation to the floor, walls, ceiling, or other surroundings that have been selected for the performance?

You can look for story in dance—though not all pieces are narrative. Those that use story carry repetitions and reexaminations that can take you on a journey just as the greatest film or short story will. The same thing might be accomplished with a journey of emotion or mood. When first experiencing dance, watch for these markers and see if the dance is reaching out to you in this way.

An examination of negative space can also be of great interest. Negative space is all of the space in which there is not a body. Thus, if the show is on a stage that has walls around it like a box, the negative space is all of the space that is not taken up by a body. That space will then be cut, filled, or traversed by bodies in motion. A simple thought experiment might suit us here. Imagine a large stage. Now imagine three dancers crouched together in one corner—say at the bottom right-hand side of your visual field. The bodies themselves will be interesting, but notice how all that space to the left and above them seems to weigh down on them or relates to their size and shape in space.

Sound will almost always be an important component of a dance piece. The use of audio can run the gamut from music that seems to guide the movement of the bodies, to sounds that occur on their own or in collaboration with the movement. Finally, one of the really interesting aspects of sound is the sound of the effort coming from the bodies of the dancers. The breathing, footfalls, and rushing fabrics of the dancers remind us that no matter how strong the artistic impact of the visual and aural fields, living, breathing bodies are at work.

Each performance is also an experience of its own. Within that experience you may wish to isolate individual performances, but never lose sight of the overall impact of the work.

Your task: experience some dance. If you have the ability, go to a dance show in your community. If not, watch some recorded dance. Please make sure to find some professional artists doing the work and don't just watch dance entertainment.

Science 18

There are few topics quite so broad as "Science and Creativity." Yet, for the most part, the issues in this area that we need to examine if we are to set our study of creativity on solid ground are relatively few. The reason is that scientific practice works at either the most creative of all realms of study or the least. Making sure which end you are at determines whether you are someone who will make new discoveries or someone who runs tests for others. Allow me to explain.

First, we need some simple history. Many of you will know that when we look at the earliest artists they were often also scientists. We are repeatedly told that this was because the field of knowledge was so small back then. Our current, complex environment requires us to specialize in narrow fields. This assertion does not hold. Repeatedly, we find that the most successful scientists have active creative lives. From painting and piano to funding and attending the arts, scientists are at the forefront of creative living.

Each year when I teach creativity class, I have science students come to me and ask for special help because they feel that they are not creative.

In every case I have encountered so far this has not been true. So, why do they feel this way? Popular misrepresentation.

Allow me to make a rather large suggestion. I think that scientists are actually closer in their work to the work of artists than any other group. Why? Because both are committed to relentless inquiry in the name of discovery, and neither will allow themselves to fall prey to an absolute truth. They are committed to maintaining open minds in order to remain on the forefront of discovery. Or at least, the truly successful artists and scientists are! So where has the misunderstanding come from? It turns out that it comes from the very best of intentions.

When science is at its most powerful it is all about experimentation and discovery. It is about the production of new knowledge. At university, we call this pure science. Throughout history almost every major discovery that we have has come about as a result of pure science. Now, what this means is that we have to let the scientists muck around and make discoveries in their own way. That means that they often discover the solution to one problem when they started to examine an entirely different issue. It's the nature of discovery itself because, by definition, it is the unknown. How could anything be more creative than that?

So, here comes the problem.

Imagine that you are someone that takes a special interest in one problem facing society. What you want is for the scientists to find a solution to that problem. What do you do? You give money to the scientists and tell them to only study the problem you have identified. As I am sure you can tell, that is not going to work very well with the nature of discovery. It also means that now instead of having the most qualified person (the scientist) making the decision about the science we have you making the decisions for them. So what you have is the least-qualified person guiding a project that is using science in a way that has been proven to be the wrong way to go about things.

Who would do such a crazy thing? Actually, almost all of us would. Whether it is government or corporations, people who have an interest in a specific outcome want to control the way science works. When they try, they get poor results, but they cannot stop trying because they are committed to their cause and want to do something about it.

Of course, this is a very simple way to look at a large issue, but I think you will find that it works as a useful guide. Now, let's look at how we might maintain or even grow discovery under such conditions.

Let's say that the problem we want to solve is cancer. We want to find a cure. That sure seems like something we should want to do, right? What's the best way to go about it? Well, we can blend our approach. We can tell the scientists to work in that general area, but try and give them enough leeway that discovery can actually happen. It's hard for us to do though. Something in the way that we think will not allow us to follow the facts. We want to solve the problem so bad that sometimes we will focus too much on one tiny area of the problem at the expense of true discovery.

One solution that a lot of people have talked about is the percentage rule. Under this model, you take a certain percentage of time each week and tell employees that they are free to work on anything they want. You just give them the materials they need and they go wild. It sounds like a lot of fun, no? It also turns out to be incredibly productive because, as you guessed, it gets us back to pure research.

Universities were first designed to be places for pure research. The big picture idea was that government would take care of organization, police and military would take care of security, the legal system would take care of justice, and universities would conduct research that would feed society with new ideas and discoveries. As you can tell, that's almost a perfect recipe for creativity. Yet, many people argue that schools kill creativity. How could that be?

Again, what we find are people with really good intentions trying to control the outcomes of ideas. We know that it will not work, but they just cannot help themselves wanting to try and make the world work out the way they want. So, here's the lesson: if you want to work in the sciences and you find yourself in an area that does not allow for pure research, you are not going to be getting your creativity from your work. Sure, you can find ways to increase your creativity during your day-to-day experience, but if you really want to work creatively, you need to get into the world of discovery.

Now we need to take a moment and come at this from another side. I mentioned previously that when I teach creativity classes, science students often wonder if they are creative. The same problem happens in the opposite direction. Often, students in the arts just assume that they are being creative. It is not necessarily so. In fact, just as I instruct the biochemists to go and see some dance our dancers need to study some biology, chemistry, and physics. Remember that whatever area is your comfort zone might always be your area of expertise, but if you want to expand your creative potential you need to work the muscles that have been lying dormant.

What can you do to wake those muscles up? Well, our good friends the scientists actually work pretty hard to publish their research in magazines that almost anyone can read. There is a caution here to which you need to pay special attention. In my experience there are two things that drive scientists nuts. One is having non-experts try and influence their work, as I just described; and the other is having non-experts report their findings in a way that does not accurately represent the nature of their discovery. You can see this happening every time a sensational news story comes out about a new medical breakthrough.

Too often we end up with years worth of work being summed up in a handful of words that are being used not to accurately represent the true nature of the work, but instead to draw attention to the reporter or news story. What this means is that you have to go the extra mile if you want to become a little more literate in the world of science. And how could you not be? We live in one of the most exciting ages yet known to our species. To turn your back on science is to accept a life that is only partially lived. What this means is that we need to develop our own scientific skills of non-judgmental inquiry. The minute that you try and read only the science that supports what you want to believe is the minute you have stopped being creative. Keep an open mind and worry about solving problems once the work of pure research is under way.

Let me return briefly to an unpopular assertion of mine. I often find that students will just block this out after I have said it. So, I'll say it again. If you got an education that let you stop taking math before you were done you have been robbed. When I was young, students used to say, "what will I need geometry or statistics for?" The answer is twofold: first you will need it to understand the science that can feed and nurture your creativity, and second it grows parts of your brain that will otherwise lie dormant. That's a polite way of saying that without math you will have lower mental function. Not a bad reason to bang away at those math skills if you ask me.

The final thing that we need to discuss about scientific work is the nature of scale. Allow me to give you an example. If I learn how to blow a whistle I can practice it for a long time and make it do some interesting things. If I want to learn to play piano it is going to take a little longer before I can reach a level of proficiency. Certain scientific disciplines are like learning the piano. It can take a lot of years of work learning the necessary scales to become someone who can really play, but it is well worth the wait.

Your task: write out your understanding of the definition of scientific discovery in one paragraph.

Visual Culture

The study of visual culture has come a long way over the past few decades, but it still has quite a journey to go. This chapter will attempt to introduce readers to something that is almost inherently non-textual and that may well be of greater importance than traditional literacy.

In a rather ironic twist, I want to begin with a story in order to arrive at the place we need to be in order to discuss visual culture. On December 28, 2005, I was attending a meeting of the Modern Language Association (MLA) in Washington, D.C. The annual conference of the MLA brings together scholars and advanced students working on all matters textual. On this particular day, I went to see the presentation of a lifetime achievement award to J. Hillis Miller. Miller was one of the most important critics of the latter twentieth century and continues to do fascinating work.

The reason that I want to share this story is because of what Miller said when he accepted his award. He told the group that really the book was becoming a thing of the past. He explained that people of his generation got most of their stories from books. There was some challenge from radio, but the majority of story you would encounter in a lifetime came from the written word read from a book, magazine, or newspaper.

Film changed everything. Whether in terms of the photograph, television, or motion pictures, film changed the way we receive stories. But that is not all. What is truly fascinating is that now it seems that film has been surpassed, too. Digital technology is rapidly replacing all previous forms of media in the realm of storytelling.

Of course this will not be news to you. Most people who read this will have received far more information from film and the Internet than they have from books. That's a big shift. No matter what part of the shift we look at, though, what is apparent is that the visual realm has become far more important while at the same time the textual realm has seen a decrease in influence.

Doesn't it seem strange then that we continue to teach students to read long novels but do not offer required classes in the interpretation, creation, and discussion of visual information? If the idea of literacy was to allow us to make informed choices about the world in which we live, it would seem that we are derelict in our duty if we do not begin to pursue organized, long-term study of visual media. In other words, students should be studying film and multimedia arts throughout their careers. That does not mean showing them a film about media but studying the film as an expression on its own terms. And once we deal with that we need to spend some serious time on the world of digital media.

Specialists in education tell us that as many as fifty percent of learners are visual learners. That is, they learn more readily through the visual medium than through text. Imagine what it will mean to those students if we start to speak to them in the language in which they are strongest. And what will it mean to those that have only been trained in traditional, textual practice?

Of course artists that work with visual media are already well schooled in these areas, but most of us stop studying art and such things at a very early age. That is a crime. In a world that is increasingly dominated by visual expression we need to study visual art as a means of developing the communication skills necessary to perform in the world in which we now live. The problem for those of you reading this book when it first comes out is that you are going to need to take care of this challenge yourself.

The reason that you are on your own is that our educational system is taking too long to make these changes. Why, you ask? It's not their fault. You may recall that we talked in the last chapter about folks in government and corporations that like to try and guide science to solve the world's problems? Well, they do the same thing with education. The problem is that right now we are going through the biggest technological change in the history of the world, and the folks running the government and big business are from a generation that exists on the other side of the digital divide. In simple terms, they do not get it. What that means is that whenever they talk about education they talk about getting back to the basics and getting more rigorous with tests and things.

Often you will hear people talking about not wanting computers in the classroom. That's a great idea if you are going to graduate and then get into a time machine and head back to the nineteenth century, but otherwise it's just plain silly. That old world is gone and the new world—your world—is visually rich.

Okay, so enough of my ranting about the change. No wait, let me take that back. I want to say one more thing on the subject. Very often you will hear people talking about the big changes coming in the digital revolution. We need to get past that—the world has already changed. We are in the new world, so let's start behaving like it. Ahhh, that feels better. Now I can go on.

So, in the case of visual culture, we need to understand that to improve our creative practice we face two challenges. The first is that the world has shifted dramatically towards visual information and, as such, we are soaked in visual messages every day. The second challenge is that very few people are paying attention to this reality. What can we do given the current reality? The answer is to attempt to develop our own visual awareness.

A lot of programs suggest starting by keeping a visual diary. Just for a week, try to note the major visual messages you encounter in a day. This list could include everything from a corporate logo at your school to a film to the way a certain homepage is laid out. Doing this has the effect of waking us up to the amount of visual information that is coming at us every day. Once we go through a waking up process then it's time to find ways to get a little more informed about visual culture. Do it without text.

Let's begin by looking at a few ways that visual culture might be sending us simple messages. During an average week do you see any visual images of people where the purpose of the message is to have you compare your appearance with theirs? If so, why is that comparison being made? What is the effect of the comparison on you?

Following the same line of inquiry, during an average week, do you see any shows, programs, films, or clips that represent people living their lives in such a way that you are invited to compare the way they live with the way you live? Is the comparison positive? Negative? A bit of both? Why is this comparison being drawn? What is the effect of it on your life?

During an average week do you see any images—from logos, to pictures, to posters, programs, and films—that represent organizations? What do the visuals say about the organization with which they are affiliated? Why are they using these visuals to send that message? What is the effect on your life?

During an average week how often is your image captured? Are you filmed at work? Do you go to the mall? Are you on a university campus? Does your city have closed circuit television monitoring? Why is your image being captured? How is it being used? What is the effect on your life?

Finally, in an average week how often do you express yourself visually? Do you use symbols rather than text in any of your communications? Do you post photos of yourself? Of friends? Of places? Of things you like? What message are you trying to send? To whom are you speaking? What do you think the effect is on the people to whom you are projecting these images?

The reason that we want to ask all of these questions is that we have a right to engage with our world on its own terms. If I try to write a message to you or deliver a speech about a given subject you are probably pretty well prepared to evaluate my argument because you have been brought up doing reading comprehension and other such things. But what about visual comprehension? How are you supposed to make informed choices about information if we never talk about visual culture?

Visual culture is the world of images in which we live. We are awash in a continually growing field of visual information that is growing in size and complexity every day. In order to live creative lives in this climate you will need to begin to expand your visual skills. That can mean studying traditional art, looking into architecture, film, photography, or game design. It can mean merely becoming more aware of the way in which our world is shifting towards visual expression. It seems like a daunting task, but it is not. We are already living in the richest visual field of all time; all we need to do now is to strengthen our awareness a bit so that we can really fully appreciate the world in which we live.

Your task: keep a visual journal for a week.

New Literacy

In the last chapter, we looked at waking up our visual comprehension skills. Now, we need to expand that concept in order to examine another trend that is here to stay. In earlier parts of this book we have examined some of the fundamental art forms that have been around for thousands of years. Art, dance, theatre, music, and sculpture are disciplines with illustrious histories. We also looked at science and talked about the way in which scientists often are artists or art enthusiasts. All of this has been done from our twenty-first century perspective and all of it is incredibly important for our studies.

What we are attempting to do is broaden our skills when it comes to sending, receiving, and processing information in order to allow ourselves to reach our creative potential. Now, we must confront one of the most exciting developments in the creative field—multidisciplinary arts. Actually, even using the term *multidisciplinary* is a bit out of date at this juncture. Let us talk instead of post-disciplinary arts.

Since earliest time, creative people have worked with others on projects that defy easy categorization. It is easy to understand these types of projects when we look at the earliest creators who saw work in the arts and sciences as part of the same work. One of the most important effects of recent changes in our world has been the return to a rich exploration of these same types of projects but with advanced technological support.

The forces fueling these projects are the same three areas that we discussed at the outset of the book. Brain sciences are causing various groups to reach across old boundaries to come together and realize the benefits of the new research in human cognition. Globalization is bringing together people from diverse backgrounds in a way that causes an inherent blending of flavors and textures and causes creators to dream up new ways of cross-pollinating work. Finally, supporting and driving it all is the realm of new technology that allows us to more readily blend, manipulate, and share creations that come from many sources. It is an incredibly exciting time to be alive.

Given the various possibilities that these new conditions afford, how can we best prepare ourselves to take advantage of the new vistas that are continually opening up? The answer is in the development of new literacy.

Let's look at what we think of literacy. In past generations, we spoke about literacy as being an essential component of being a citizen. The idea was that if you were able to read you could evaluate the information that made up your society and that would, in turn, allow you to participate fully in the way that it operated. To a lesser extent we spoke also of numeracy. That is, fluency with basic mathematics. Now what we are seeing is something well beyond those simple, earlier formulations.

The last chapter argued that we need to develop visual literacy. But surely, you might ask, there will be other literacies? Such as aural (or sound based) literacy? After all, we have a lot of scientific evidence telling us about the benefits of musical education, and there is also an awful lot of sonic information coming to us through sound in film, television, and new media.

The answer is that we need a new literacy that is greater than the sum of its parts. To be that, however, it must have good quality parts with which to begin. Why don't we take a crack at developing a new literacy that might help us better educate ourselves for the twenty-first century? It should be fun, but we need to keep two things in mind. First, what we are creating is an ideal; it will require significant work to implement; and, second, if you are reading this, no matter what happens it will never be ready in time to train you, so it will be up to you to take responsibility for this in your own life. Here we go:

1. Literacy—as much as we have been talking about the falling stock of textual literacy, it is still of primary importance. Two major items must get your attention. You want the good one or the bad one first? The good news is this—we need to ease up on people who text and email all kinds of very casual writing. It is a new way of communicating, and it is every bit as legitimate as any other form. The bad news is that you also must train yourself for the type of extended-form reading that can only come from a long novel. It's good for your brain, and what's good for your brain is good for your creativity. If it's hard for you to read long books, that is proof that you need practice. Reading, like almost everything else, gets easier with practice.

2. Numeracy—we've known for years that we do a lousy job of teaching mathematics in our schools. The good news is there are a lot of folks posting work online that gets around this problem. Math is essential to your work, no matter what work you do. If anyone ever tries to give you an education that excludes math you should run in the opposite direction.

3. Visual—as we discussed in the last chapter, we have to get better at engaging in visual culture. We are already living in a visual age; it's about time our discussion caught up to this wonderfully rich area of discovery and allowed us to actually participate in our world.

4. Musical—there is a mountain of evidence that tells us that musical education will help us function better in every area of our lives. Expensive private schools all have music programs. Poor ones don't. Do you really think those private schools would be offering music if it didn't matter? It doesn't matter how good you are, working on music will make you more creative.

5. Physical—there are many ways to go about becoming physically literate. Dance may well be the best one, but there are others. There is one important thing to watch for here, though—you are not going to become more physically literate by running up and down carrying heavy things. A lot of our physical education programs were designed to tire students out so they will not misbehave. Doing so is the opposite of creative practice; it will actually make you less creative. Find something that moves your body in a way that requires complicated, refined movement. It might be ballet or it might be karate.

6. Virtual—the computer age has opened up new worlds of exploration. Virtual worlds are nearly endless in their possibilities. We can create almost anything that we can dream up, but you can't dream up very much if you do not know how to work and live in the new virtual universe. Start spending time in virtual environments that require creative engagement. If what you are doing is a time-wasting thing where you have no input in how the world operates, then you are not being creative. You need to find tools

that will allow you to begin to express your imagination in a virtual way.

7. Emotional—for decades now experts have been telling us that we need to spend more time on our emotional intelligence. At school we continue to ignore it because of a bias towards a type of neutral, gray mood that is supposed to be the most conducive to academic work. That's ridiculous. Develop your emotional palette, and your world gets better. You may have guessed by now that one of the best ways to do this is to get in touch with your creative aptitudes.

So there we have it—our ideal set of literacies. Now what I want you to do is imagine that you could "speak" all of these seven languages. The result of developing all of these skills will not just be the addition of seven new ways of working. You will realize benefits that are beyond the sum of all of these parts. New literacy is about a quantum leap forward in the way that we think, feel, and create.

I now want to give you one important warning and one suggestion. The warning involves being lazy with your literacy. You will recall from the start of the book that Plato worried about the artist not being an expert in anything, stealing instead from all of those who truly had what he called techné. If you try to take a shortcut to literacy you run the risk of being one of these people. The best route to creativity is through developing a solid set of literacies.

Finally, before I finish this chapter, I want to lobby for my own little world. If you look at all of the literacies described, you will find that they are all needed in the theatre. Theatre is one of the oldest disciplines, but it is also one of the richest and most welcoming. When it is done properly it has the ability to expose one to a myriad of new possibilities, some actual and some virtual. Okay, that's my little advertisement!

Your task: Look at the list of seven literacies. Rank them in order of strength in your life from the one you are strongest at to the weakest. Begin to make a plan to find more balance.

Video/Computer Games

Now that we have established the broad spectrum of literacy that will serve our creative potential best, it is time to move into the art forms that currently dominate our culture and seem poised to do so for years to come. Public opinion on video games runs a wide range but seems to separate people into two broad categories. I want to look at those two groups and argue that we will actually find our place somewhere in the middle.

First, I want to be clear about a position that underlies all of the work I talk about in this book. It is important to understand that we are currently living in a world that is undergoing the largest single change in communication and information technology in the history of the world. Moreover, much of this change has already occurred and so we are actually now living in the first moments of a changed world sharing the planet with those raised in the past age as well as those born fresh into the new one.

The forces of this special time are of particular interest for those studying creativity. The reason is that we see over and over that creativity thrives when left alone to find its own means of expression. Trying to forcefully induce innovation or discovery simply does not work. Why does this matter for the digital shift? Allow me to explain with a question.

If what I am asserting is true and we are experiencing the biggest single shift in communication in history, what would we expect to see? We should see some people that become enamored with the new technology and go after it in a fevered pitch. On the opposite side of the spectrum we should expect to see people from the previous generation crying out in a form of repressed fear about the dangers of the new technology. That's exactly what happened centuries ago when the printing press was introduced in Europe. Scholars called that transition the incunabular period. My argument is that we are in a second incunabulum and that this one is far greater in scope than the first.

Now, if you accept these assertions, here is what comes out for those of us interested in creativity. There are two groups that frame this new world. The first group is those raised under the old system. They did not grow up with computers and they are understandably frightened by new technology. Some of them will go so far as to reject email and computers all together. If my theory is right, these folks are the last of their kind. Once they die, a population that has always known digital technology will replace them. Think of it is a form of evolution if you like.

Folks that are of this school tend to attack digital media by talking about the misuses of smart phones, overuse of the Internet, and the mind-numbing effects of video games. These same types of warnings came out from the older generation who were around when printing presses made printed words widely available to the populations of Europe. What happened? Were minds ruined? No. Literacy expanded and flourished.

So, what can we expect this time? Remember our last chapter?

The second category is the tech-obsessive group who seems no longer to live in this world. These folks are so far gone into the technology that they have lost all perspective. Some people argue that this is okay, but in reality these people are incredibly vulnerable if we ever experience a power outage because their reality requires a constant power supply.

Of course, both of these areas are extreme, but we can expect such polarization as a result of the magnitude of the changes that are happening. In reality, most of us will find ourselves in the middle of these two groups and our choices will determine where on the scale we will find ourselves.

What is important for this book is to ask where on that sliding scale is the best space for the creative person? I would like to argue that you should be closer to the tech folks than the old school lobby. The reason is that we live in an increasingly digital world and to deny that is to deny reality. In fact, the digital shift is one of the biggest forces pushing creative energy right now. At the same time its effects are also manifesting a need for us to be creative beings in order to adapt.

To pick up my evolution analogy, that theory tells us it is not a case of the strongest or the most social beings surviving. It is those who are most able to adapt. The ability to move with change is what allows us to thrive under new circumstances.

Please think about the consequences of this argument for a moment. If the world really is going through the biggest change in its history, and the only way to survive is to emphasize and enhance our ability to adapt, then to work on our creativity may be the single greatest survival technique that we can use to live in the twenty-first century.

So what does this have to do with computer games? Everything. Here's the thing, if you are not currently playing computer games you need to start right away. If you are already playing games you need to evaluate your game play and tweak it so that it best serves your creative expression.

The trick here is that you want to get away from time-wasting games that do little other than lull you into a semi-conscious state and towards those games that challenge your problem-solving skills, your virtual communication and interaction skills, and at the best, that allow you to become the creator of new material using the powerful new tools that are available to those who wish to express themselves. Think of it this way— the designers of games create challenges that give you the illusion of choice. You think you can choose one path or another, but really the world-builder is the one that has the most choice. Do whatever you can to move towards becoming one of those world-builders.

Does this mean that everyone should become a game designer? Yes and No. Yes in the sense that everyone should attempt to benefit from the incredibly rich palette that is available to the artist that works in this medium. No, in that you do not need to actually do this as a job or build a standalone game. What is important is that you understand the language. Video games are replacing books, television, and film as the dominant means of sharing narrative in our society. If you decide, "oh, games are not for me, I will only read books" then you are deciding to live in the past. It's your call.

Rejecting technology is not necessarily a bad thing. Throughout history there have been small groups of people that turned away from technology and left society to follow their views. What I am asserting is that at this particular time in history you have a big choice to make. Either you are in or you are out. My caution is that if you reject the digital world, I firmly believe that you are going to have a very difficult time thriving in the twenty-first century.

When we do brain scans of those that live highly wired lives their brains look different from those who follow the old book-reading-only model. Do you realize what that means? It means that the current generation has fundamentally different brains than the last. That is an incredible shift. No wonder then that we will have people screaming and crying over the dangers of the digital world and no wonder that those people cannot seem to make digital technology work. Their brains simply do not have the appropriate wiring.

So what do we look for in a game when we want to do a creative evaluation? As I mentioned, the most important component is the nature of choice. If you are just starting out with games you are not going to be able to worry about this too much right away. At first, you just need to get used to the interface. The type of literacy that you need to play games involves a different way of thinking and a certain type of physical dexterity that can be improved upon with practice.

There are too many different kinds of games to do summaries of them all here, but once you have a decent facility with the games you want to evaluate the nature of choice in the game. If the game is merely a flash and push game—that is, one that involves little more than quickly pushing buttons in response to bursts of light and colour—you won't be doing much other than training the simplest part of your brain. You might get some hand-eye coordination benefits, but the cognitive impact is not great.

Where games get exciting is when they allow you to develop problem-solving skills. Moving in space and beginning to understand three-dimensional mapping and to then extend that to multi-player collaborative work is a wonderfully creative avenue to pursue. Once you get to that level of fluency what you really want to do is get to a stage where you can begin to make changes to the game or to program your own game or components of a game. This sounds daunting, but it is not. It can be learned a little at a time like painting, writing, or dancing. We are in the age of games—are you in or out?

Your task: do a game analysis. Keep your eyes open for creative options in various games. Move your game play gradually in a creative direction.

Creativity Online

It is hard to imagine a world more suited to creative pursuits than the world that is now available to us online. Yet, at the same time, there are ways in which we can engage with the online universe that can rob us of the flexibility necessary to be creative. What we find is that the same tensions, between the old and the new, exist in the online world. As the old group attempts to control the Internet and its related systems, they make the mistake of trying to organize information in the manner of book culture. For those growing up in this world, the very idea of control of information is anathema.

At the outset of this book, I mentioned that work on creativity is inherently amoral. It really can benefit anyone in his or her work and does not require a particular position or ideology. That said, what is very clear to all who study or practice creative performance is that the free flow of information is key. That is why this is such an exciting time to be alive. It is also why we need to help older individuals understand that when they try to lock down or govern information they are choking the creative future of their children and grandchildren.

What does creativity look like online? The answer is too vast to comprehend. What is clear is that our minds are changing in order to live in a digital world. If you want to remain creative within this climate you need to do everything you can to keep access to information entirely open and to make your ability to interpret and use that information continually increase. More than that, though, you need to recognize that we are thinking differently now. That is not good or bad, it just is. This world is the one in which you live, and we need to engage our creativity in the world as we know it.

So, let's look at what types of things might impede or enhance our creativity when it intersects with our online lives. When we started the book we determined that creativity had to do with creating *new* things that have *value*. The two italicized terms cause us a bit of trouble when we try to agree on their definitions, but our overall formulation works quite well.

The next thing we know is that the more raw materials we have the better. It allows us to have a greater horizon of possible combinations with which to create new things that have value. Once we have those raw materials, we then need to be able to work with them in a meaningful way. Think about someone who is given a warehouse filled with all the car parts in the world. If they don't know how to make a car, all those raw materials are going to go to waste.

There is really only one issue when it comes to impeding your access to raw materials to fuel your creativity, but there are two components with which we must deal. The issue is access to information or, in more popular terms, freedom of speech. Freedom of information literally refers to the amount of raw materials you have at your disposal. The only way to limit it is for someone to decide what you can and cannot see. You will recall from the earlier part of this book that Plato felt our society would be better if most people were told what they could and could not experience, while Aristotle felt that we would be improved by greater interaction with information. Never has this argument had more saliency than now in what many call the "information age."

The other way that we can impede your access to information is through technology. Some people have great computers and networks and some people have none. If I give you access to information, I can help you to realize your creative potential. If I do not, you will not have that opportunity. Now, most of us think right away that full access for everyone would be a great idea—it would literally give us more access to more ideas thereby guaranteeing greater chances for creative flourishing. But remember our point about the amorality of creativity. Some people are going to do things with that access that you may not like. Perhaps they speak against your government, your company, you as a person, or perhaps they will use it to try and cause bodily harm. These are important considerations. If you are on the side of creativity you have to support access to information, but how far you go is up to you.

The one complicating factor is history. As we discussed, this is a very particular time in societal development. The change to digital culture in a global context is the largest shift in the way people think and communicate on record. The positive side of that means that we get to live in very exciting times and to access avenues of creativity never before available. The negative side is that too often those who are in power in governments and companies are simply unaware of what computers and networks actually do. As a result, we get bizarre spending that directs money to areas that would not get funding if computer literate people were making the decisions.

Allow me to be blunt. When we look at populations throughout history we repeatedly see the trend that as people get older they grow increasingly cautious and resistant to change. In the past, we have talked about this in terms of things such as a "generation gap" where the older people criticize younger people's manners or style of clothing and music. But now, at the time of this great shift in the way the world thinks and communicates, many in the older generation do not possess the ability to understand what is going on around them. Those that have refused to train themselves in new technology, that wish to sit out during the biggest change in history, have opted out of understanding this new world in the hopes that they can finish their lives under old models. That would not be too much of a problem if they sat quietly on the sidelines while the world moved on, but these are the folks that are in charge of our governments and our companies.

Okay, so before my younger readers get too high and mighty about the fact that they are part of the most exciting generation so far, let's make sure we are clear about what we are saying here. Anyone who decides to sit out the advances that we are making is making a huge decision. For some, the changes are simply too new, and they would prefer to spend their remaining days living in the past. For those born into this era, a decision not to become aware of digital culture borders on insanity. At the very least, it is just about the worst career decision I can imagine. Age doesn't matter, change does.

In an earlier chapter, I made the point that we need to get past the idea that change is coming and accept that the world has already changed. Here's an example of why. To my students I am an old guy. My dad, then, who is no longer alive, must seem ancient. Yet, he put himself through university working on IBM computers for an automaker. That was in the 1960s! Anyone who thinks that the computer age is new is dreaming. So when I talk about older folks who don't want to accept technology, I am only talking about a general trend. Many of my teachers who are far more adept at digital technology than me are older than I am, and some of my students who are much younger are nearly ignorant of these changes.

The reason that we want to be aware of this trend is that it can negatively impact your creativity if you let it. Here's why. Over the past number of years governments and large organizations have poured money into projects that use computers. Why did they do it? Because they know that computers are the future, and they know that if they don't support new projects they will look like they are out of date. The problem is that if the people sending out the money don't understand the language of the digital age they will not know how to pick the right programs. It's a good way to waste a lot of money.

One last note on impediments. Do you recall our discussion about science and creativity? In that chapter, we discussed the fact that any time governments or corporations try to control how discovery works it actually impairs our ability to be creative. The same thing goes for digital technology, except now, not only are they wrong to try and control creativity, in many cases they do not even understand the world they are trying to govern. Sound scary? It's not. Or at least, it's not for you. For them, it is very scary, and we can expect them to yell and shout about the dangers of the future, the dangers of open access, and the dangers of discovery. For creative people, the only response is to maintain the greatest possible input of raw materials and move on.

But what do we do with all of that information? Once we have access to infinite information won't we drown if we do not know how to handle it? Of course we will. Or, at least, we would if we had not already taken steps to prepare ourselves. Look back over the chapters of this book. Developing your literacy on a variety of fronts, stretching your creativity by attending arts events, having other experiences that are outside of your regular realm of experience, and taking control of your life in order to keep yourself free enough to benefit from creativity will leave you perfectly prepared to handle the exciting new frontiers of the digital age. Developing new literacies guarantees success.

Your task: list three ways that others try to control your access to information, then list three ways that your access to information is improved.

Conclusion

At the opening to this book I promised you that it would be simple. I feel quite confident that I have lived up to that commitment! You will no doubt have noticed that this is not designed to be a traditional, academic book. You may even have picked up on the fact that the reason for this book's format relates to the arguments that are lying at the heart of the chapters you just read.

What I hope we have done is to start a conversation. The more we learn about the way humans work, the more we come to understand that many minds will always outperform the singular consciousness. By promoting and maintaining conversations with as many people from as many backgrounds as possible we cannot help but find new ideas around every corner.

Yet, at the same time that we must celebrate the wisdom of the crowd, creativity remains a private practice. What you do to expand your own creative abilities is entirely up to you. It is clear through years of study and debate that we will always be working to improve education and the way in which it can help us be better versions of ourselves, but at this time—perhaps more than any other time in history—you are on your own. Schools, governments, and companies simply cannot change fast enough to respond to the needs you have.

Your life will be lived in the creative age. Whether or not you participate is up to you. What I wish I could get through to you, more than any other thing in this book, is that if you fail to develop your own strengths and weaknesses it will be very challenging for you to survive in a world of near global competition.

But the news is good.

You live in the best time ever. Take advantage of it. Start today and make creativity a priority in your life. It will take time and it will take effort, but the changes that you make can be done in short little bursts, rather than in massive, overwhelming challenges.

If you are looking for specific instruction on how to get started, consider this example. Researchers tell us that in order to create a habit we need to do something every day for about twenty-one to thirty days. So, just to be on the safe side, go with thirty. We also know that if you attempt some massive change, it will be hard for you to keep it up. What that means is that if you want to affect change in your life as part of your creativity plan you should experiment with something that is easy to add. Why not come up with something that takes five minutes a day? Do it for thirty days and give it an honest try. Look at the results. If it works then you have got some great motivation to expand your practice. If it doesn't work, you really haven't lost all that much. If the stakes are as high as I am arguing, it's a pretty good bet to make.

What does a good creative practice look like? Why don't we finish with an ideal example that you can use for a thought experiment? What matters and what doesn't?

1. Male/female/gender. Does not matter. One thing we do know is that if you are working in a system that values the ideas of some people more than others you will be less creative. Remember, more ideas from more people is all that matters.

2. Race, ethnicity, etc. Does not matter. Just like gender, all that matters is ideas. The only thing that can help is if you can work with people from a variety of perspectives since that increases the spectrum of ideas.

3. Religion. Does not matter. You can be any faith or no faith, as long as you are open-minded and are ready to share information.

4. Profession. Does not matter. You might be working in a dull, repetitive job or you might be a poet. Unless you are working on your creativity your job title does not matter.

5. Journal. Matters. Do it. We know that people that keep journals outperform those that do not. Get serious about it, though. Try to record things that will challenge your current skills and ignite new ones.

6. Arts events. Matter. Go to them. Try to get to one new challenging event each week. If you can't do that, do it once a month. Consider this as nourishing your creative system. And, remember, don't try to "understand" everything—if you see something that confuses the heck out of you that might just be the best thing you can do. The one note to this is that if you are already seeing a lot of arts you may need to go to more science-oriented events to support your creative work. You will know which direction is the right one. When you attend an event, write down your impressions in your journal.

7. Arts practice. Matter. Do them. Take up painting or a musical instrument. Learn to dance with your partner, or go on your own.

Better yet, do all of these things, and recognize that when you do them you are not wasting time, you are investing in your most valuable asset: yourself. You are the only thing you can count on in the creative age. Take care of yourself and always work at improvement.

8. Education. Matters. Don't leave it up to others. Schools do a lot of things very well, but changing quickly is not one of them. Given that you live in a time of incredible change you need to take the reins of your own education or you are going to be woefully unprepared. And let's be clear what woefully unprepared means—you won't have any work, and it will be hard to buy food.

9. Other people's ideas. Matter. Listen to them. Those that have open minds will rule the future; those that keep repeating the same thing and that only listen to arguments that support what they already believe are turning themselves into whiny automatons that we can easily replace with a computer that won't yell so much.

10. Your ideas. Matter. Challenge them. Journaling is not enough. You need to remember that creative thought requires you to actively challenge your own ideas. The best way to do that is to pick one idea every day and to flesh out what you believe and why you believe it. The exercise will expand your powers of cognition. Want an example? Do you believe the world is round? Why? Did you do the studies yourself? (I know, this seems silly, but we fill our heads with ideas that we "believe," and if we are to be creative we need to examine all of them.)

11. Context. Matters. Dump boring friends and move out of restrictive social groups. Sounds kind of scary? Good. That's what creativity feels like. Stasis feels comfortable. So does death.

12. Emotion. Matters. Take care to go easy on those you work with. It will help them to be more comfortable and to be more willing to share ideas that will help you in your work. Most importantly, though, learn to go easy on yourself. As much as this book argues that you should work to improve your creative skills it does not advocate pushing yourself so hard that you are exhausted. Tired people do not create as well as those that are healthy. Most importantly, work on your human connections.

Finally, please ensure that you go easy on yourself as you find your way into the creative age. There are a lot of people out there that are shouting at us that the new age is moving faster and is getting more competitive than ever. They tell us that the world is a frightening place. They are dead wrong. The world is a beautiful place, and you will do incredibly well if you just follow along in your own creative way. Take care to develop the skills that you have, and no one can ever out compete you. We each have the ability to be the very best version of ourselves possible. To do that, we need to tap into our creativity, but we do not need to drive ourselves to collapse. One of the biggest lessons that we must learn is to take care of ourselves. Be kind to your mind, body, and spirit. You will be far more creative if you feel good. Try to avoid the silly old trap that makes us think that we are being better people if we work long hours every day. In fact, you will be far more productive if you work smarter and more creatively for fewer hours.

Thank you for taking the time to read this book. The final thing that I wish to say is that you should not take anything I say at face value. Try it out for yourself. I think you will be convinced, but only you can be the judge. Good luck!